A RICH DAD ADVISO

ABCs OF BUYING RENTAL PROPERTY

HOW YOU CAN ACHIEVE
FINANCIAL FREEDOM IN FIVE YEARS

A RICH DAD ADVISOR BOOK

ABCs OF BUYING RENTAL PROPERTY

HOW YOU CAN ACHIEVE FINANCIAL FREEDOM IN FIVE YEARS

KEN McELROY

FOREWORD BY ROBERT KIYOSAKI

RDA PRESS

Published by RDA Press

Rich Dad Advisors, B-I Triangle, CASHFLOW Quadrant and other Rich Dad marks are registered trademarks of CASHFLOW Technologies, Inc.

RDA Press LLC
15170 N. Hayden Road
Scottsdale, AZ 85260
480-998-5400

Learn more at: KenMcElroy.com
                RichDad.com

Printed in the United States of America
First Edition: September 2020

ISBN: 978-1-947588-12-7

092020

Contents

Foreword

The Definition of Intelligence

Kenny and I met during the great Flipper Fest. The real estate Flipper Fest played out between the years 1997 and 2007. You know you are in a Flipper Fest when you're standing in line at a supermarket and the checkout clerk, now a Realtor®, hands you his or her business card—winking, nodding, and saying "Call me"—while they're bagging your groceries.

During the decade-long Flipper Fest, Kim and I explained to countless people, "We do not flip real estate property. We are real estate investors."

I remember walking through the Phoenix airport when a woman recognized me and said, "I have a 3-bedroom / 2-bath house I just bought for $86,000. If you give me $5,000 cash, I'll let you have it."

"And what would I do with it?" I asked her.

She looked at me like I had holes in my head, saying, "Flip it."

"I don't flip real estate," I replied politely.

"And I thought you were a big-time real estate investor," she said to me, sneering indignantly. Her parting shot: "You're just like everyone else... a big fat phony."

Meeting Ken McElroy was the "proverbial breath of fresh air." My wife Kim and I nearly cried when Ken said, "I don't flip real estate either." And when Ken followed those words with "I invest for cash flow," we knew we had found a partner.

My favorite definition for the word intelligence, *"If you agree with me... you are intelligent."* That made Ken McElroy, in our minds, the most intelligent person in the world.

When a person quickly flips a house, they are subject to ordinary income taxes. If they do enough 'flips,' payroll taxes are added on. When investing for *cash flow*, an educated real estate investor can invest for both lower capital gains taxes *and* cash flow and pay little to nothing in taxes, legally.

An educated cash flow investor also knows how to flip a property and minimize (if not avoid entirely) "flipper" taxes... legally. An uneducated "flipper" will likely always pay the highest taxes.

Since the day we met, Ken, Kim, and I have acquired numerous apartment complexes across the southwestern United States, totaling over seven thousand rental units at a cost of over a half billion dollars—using OPM, debt financing—earning us millions a year in income, with most of that income tax free.

On the day we met Ken, not only did Kim and I meet a very intelligent person, we gained a business partner, a fellow teacher, and a lifelong friend.

Almost every week, someone will approach me and say, "Because of your books, I am getting into real estate."

And, whenever I hear those words, I smile, thank them for saying "hello" and reading my books. I also warn them: "Be careful. Invest in your financial education before investing in real estate."

Unfortunately, rarely do I have the time to explain why I say, "Be careful." The following are a few of the reasons for my warnings—and why I encourage everyone to invest first in their real estate education, before they invest in real estate.

Real Estate is the **best investment** in the world, in my opinion, for the following reasons:

1. Real estate is about investing with debt, or OPM: Other People's Money.
2. Real estate can generate cash flow income for years.
3. It's likely you could pay little if anything in taxes.
4. We can find opportunities and buy more real estate when markets crash, often acquiring the properties of flippers.

Real Estate is the **worst investment** in the world for the following reasons:

1. **Real Estate is illiquid.** That means, if you make a mistake, real estate can be extremely difficult to sell or sell quickly. If you make a mistake in stocks, bonds, mutual funds, or ETFs, you can "liquidate" easily, which means you can sell quickly and cut loses almost instantly.
   If you make a mistake in real estate, you may go down with the Titanic.

2. **Real Estate is a business.** Real estate requires real business skills and a business mind. Real estate is management intensive. Many real estate dreams turn into real estate nightmares, not because real estate is bad, but because the investor's business skills are bad.

3. **Real Estate is not for "do-it-yourselfers."** Stock, bond, and mutual fund investors can get away with being "do it yourselfers." Real Estate investing is about rules, regulations, laws, records, repairs, losses, and management.
   Real estate is about debt. And debt can be a loaded gun. Debt can make you very rich or kill you.
   Real estate is a business that requires debt financing and professional management... which is why real estate investing is a team sport, played by a team of professionals. Professional real estate investors must have a bookkeeper, lawyer, accountant, and insurance agent on their team.

4. **Real Estate is about maintenance and repairs.** Real estate investors must have a handyman on call 24 hours a day, 7 days a week, unless the investor enjoys fixing toilets at midnight.

These are the reasons why Ken McElroy's real estate books, especially this book, are priceless for beginner and advanced real estate investors alike. They will teach you how to maximize the advantages of real estate investing, because I would prefer that you become a smart and rich real estate investor, rather than the captain of the SS Titanic.

These are the same reason why Ken McElroy, an expert in the field of real estate investing, is our partner, advisor, and trusted friend.

Robert Kiyosaki

Text Boxes

I use four types of text boxes to summarize key points in this book. The boxes for each type are numbered in chronological order. At the end of the book, I summarize the content in these boxes.

Fact Box: A thing that is known or proved to be true.

Definition Box: A concept or term is defined.

Tip Box: A useful piece of practical advice.

Myth Box: A widely held but false belief or idea.

Part I

How to Achieve
Financial Independence

Chapter One

A Note from Ken about Wealth

On occasion, people have likened me and some of my colleagues to the lead characters in a Horatio Alger novel.

Alger was a 19th-century American writer famous for his "rags-to-riches" stories, which chronicled the lives of impoverished boys who—through hard work, honesty, and perseverance—achieved financial security and sometimes great wealth.

I grew up in poverty.

My family never threw away anything of value, except worn shoes. My clothes were hand-me-downs. When they tore, my mother would patch them.

Today, I'm a wealthy man.

My companies control or manage nearly a billion dollars in real estate assets. I made most of my money through managing, buying, and selling rental communities.

> **Fact #1**
>
> *Horatio Alger novels promoted wealth and the American Dream.*

My wealth has given me and my family access to many wonderful things, like new clothes and vacations. I appreciate these things, perhaps more than others, because I know what it's like to be poor.

But I have never viewed wealth as an END in itself.

I don't admire my possessions like Silas Marner, the miserly character in George Eliot's novel who counted gold coins. (An orphaned girl eventually redeemed him.)

Wealth is a MEANS to an end—not the end itself.

What I cherish most about wealth isn't the things it can buy, *but the freedom it gives*—especially the freedom to spend more time with the people I love.

I visit my mother and other relatives, who live 1,700 miles away, at least eight times a year. In my free time, I also enjoy sports, writing books, and giving to charity.

> **Tip #1**
> *Wealth gives you freedom.*

Nothing is more important in life than relationships.

No amount of money can replace the love of family, friends, and colleagues. Studies even show that people on their deathbed often regret working too much and wish they had spent more time with loved ones.

Of course, I cannot guarantee you'll get wealthy after reading this or any of my other books about real estate investing.

But I can assure you that financial freedom[1] *is a very realistic goal,* and you can achieve it in five to ten years (or twenty, if you prefer to go more slowly).

> **Definition #1**
> *Financial freedom exists when your income is sufficient enough that you no longer worry about your finances.*

To achieve that freedom, you don't have be super smart (although I know you are), have a fancy education (all of life is an education), or have a lot of money (a little is helpful, especially for your first purchase). You don't even need to buy a big apartment building—you can do it one rental home or condo at a time.

To be financially independent, you just need three things: *(1) a motivation to succeed, (2) a good work ethic, and (3) a willingness to learn about real estate and from your mistakes.*

I discuss these topics in Chapter 3.

First, though, I need to convince you that real estate is one of the best and safest ways to achieve financial independence. Chapter 2 will show

---

1 Financial freedom exists when your income is sufficient enough that you no longer worry excessively about being able to pay your bills, now or in the future. Because people have different needs and goals, no dollar figure can be attached to this condition. But a necessary condition is that concerns or worries about one's financial condition will diminish.

you, using data from the U.S. Census and other governmental sources, that *real estate can routinely produce returns five times higher than the stock market.*

Then, in Chapters 4 through 13, I'll show you—through ten simple steps—how to set up a real estate business, get your investment money, find a good property to purchase, manage your property, reduce your costs, increase your revenues, build your real estate portfolio, and continue your education.

To enhance the learning process, I'll use examples and anecdotes. I'll introduce you to John, one of my acquaintances who, at age sixty-five, decided to purchase his first rental property.[2] Along the way, I'll also offer some stories about how I achieved financial independence.

> **Tip #2**
>
> *To be financially free, you need motivation, a good work ethic, and a willingness to learn.*

I offer these stories not to brag, but to convince you that:

IF JOHN AND I CAN DO IT, YOU CAN, TOO!

---

2 Although this book uses examples mostly from the United States, the steps and principles are applicable to virtually all free-market countries in the world.

Chapter Two

Why Real Estate Is a Superior Investment

There are lots of paths to financial freedom.

The fastest and easiest is to be born to rich parents.

About half of the wealth in America comes through inheritance.[3]

But if you, like me, weren't lucky enough to be born to rich parents, don't despair. We have other paths to financial freedom. We can climb (or should I say "claw") our way up the corporate ladder; invest in stocks or bonds or mutual funds; write a best-selling novel; start up a business; fix up homes; or win the lottery. Earning a top executive position in a corporation is prestigious but usually takes a long time. Stocks can be volatile.

> **Fact #2**
>
> *Being born to rich parents is the fastest way to wealth, but real estate beats all other paths.*

Bonds, annuities, and mutual funds often offer less-than-satisfactory returns. Writing a novel is hard work and only a few books make the *New York Times* best-selling list. Starting a new business is exciting but two-

---

3 See, e.g., Facundoal Varedo, Bertrand Garbinti and Thomas Piketty, "On the Share of Inheritance in Aggregate Wealth: Europe and the USA, 1900–2010," Economica (2017) 84, 239–260, retrieved 9/16/19 from http://www.piketty.pse.ens.fr/files/AlvaredoGarbintiPiketty2017.pdf and Sam Pizzigati, "The 'Self-Made' Myth: Our Hallucinating Rich," Inequality.org (September 23, 2012), retrieved 9/16/19 from https://inequality.org/research/selfmademyth-hallucinating-rich/

thirds of them fail, often leaving their owners bankrupt.[4] Fixing up homes can be lucrative, but it's a lot of hard work and your profits are heavily taxed. And the lottery—well, your odds of striking it big are 1,800 times less likely than being killed by lightning.

Each "wealth stream" has advantages over the others. (Lottery tickets are cheap, after all.)

But none has a better track record than real estate.

And to prove it, I'll first compare real estate to stock investments. Then I'll elaborate on ten financial reasons why real estate is financially superior to stocks and most other forms of investment.

A Tale of Two Investments

One of the most enduring beliefs in American culture is that the stock market beats all other investments over the long run in terms of returns. A recent story in *Forbes* magazine, for example, recommends readers invest in stocks first.[5]

> ### Myth #1
>
> *The stock market is the fastest way to wealth.*

But this is a myth.

Since 1940, the Dow Jones Industrial Average has produced an average annual return of 6.6 percent.[6] That's not bad, but it won't get you to financial freedom very quickly. If you invested $35,000 in the stock market today, it would take you fifty-two years to turn that into $1 million.

---

4 According to the Small Business Administration, cited in "Top 6 Reasons New Businesses Fail," Investopedia, retrieved 9/29/19 from https://www.investopedia.com/slide-show/top-6-reason-new-businesses-fail/

5 Jeff Rose, "7 Best Investments to Make in 2019," Forbes (Dec 27, 2018), retrieved 9/30/2019 from https://www.forbes.com/sites/jrose/2018/12/27/best-investments-2019/#24218e0869bc/ The second recommendation is real estate stock funds, which isn't the same as investing in rental properties that you own and doesn't provide the same level of return.

6 Macrotrends, retrieved 9/19/19 from https://www.macrotrends.net/1319/dow-jones-100-year-historical-chart. Since its origins in 1896, the Dow has increased an average of 5.4%, according to Zachs.com (see https://finance.zacks.com/average-return-dow-jones-during-its-lifetime-3314.html).

In contrast, a rental property produces on average a 19.2 percent return each year. A $35,000 down payment on one $140,000 rental property would generate $1 million in nineteen years.

So, if you purchase only one rental property and aren't in a hurry to reach financial freedom, you'll get there in less than twenty years.

Are you skeptical?

Good.

A savvy business person should always follow the advice of the famous French philosopher René Descartes: *All knowledge begins with doubt.*

So let me prove it to you.

I begin with two investors, each of whom has $35,000 to invest.

One puts his money into stocks, which, as I've noted earlier, increases at an average of 6.6 percent per year. Table 2.1 shows that at the end of the first year, that initial investment of $35,000 (subtracting $100 for the cost of initially placing the order to purchase the stocks through an online investment site), grows to $37,203—a $2,303 increase ($34,900 x 6.6%).

> **Definition #2**
>
> *Return on Investment (ROI) refers to the effectiveness of an investment.*

At the end of ten years (interest is compounded from year to year), the total investment grows to $66,130 ($34,900 originally invested + $31,230 in gains = $66,130). That's an 89 percent *return on investment (ROI =* [total value of investment − cost of investment] ÷ cost of investment).

That's a decent ROI.

But watch what happens when the other investor puts her money into real estate.

She purchases a $140,000 two-bedroom, two-bath single-family rental property. Three thousand dollars goes into closing costs, and the remaining $32,000 goes to the down payment.

Table 2.1 - Which Is the Better Investment: Stocks or Real Estate?
First 10 Years (Original Investment $35,000)

Column =	A	B	C	D	E
Year	Stocks Gain (6.6% Per Year)	Rental Property Gain (C+D+E)	Equity from Appreciation (6% Per Year)	Cash Flow ($275 per month x 12 = $3,300)	Equity from mortgage payments
	Investment – Costs* $34,900	Investment – Costs* $32,000	($140,000 Purchase Price)**	(5% rent increase per yr thereafter)***	(30-Year Loan at 6%)****
1	$2,303	$13,026	$8,400	$3,300	$1,326
2	$2,455	$13,777	$8,904	$3,465	$1,408
3	$2,617	$14,571	$9,438	$3,638	$1,495
4	$2,790	$15,412	$10,005	$3,820	$1,587
5	$2,974	$16,301	$10,605	$4,011	$1,685
6	$3,171	$17,242	$11,241	$4,212	$1,789
7	$3,380	$18,237	$11,916	$4,422	$1,899
8	$3,603	$19,289	$12,630	$4,643	$2,016
9	$3,841	$20,404	$13,388	$4,875	$2,141
10	$4,094	$21,584	$14,192	$5,119	$2,273
Total Gain=	$31,230	$169,843	$110,719	$41,505	$17,619
ROI=	89%	485%			
Total Value=	$66,130	$201,843			

*The interest gains for stocks are compounded. To make these findings as realistic as possible, expenses for investing were subtracted from the totals. Although the costs of investing through a stock broker can be as high as 6%, I assumed the investor invested through an online site and that it cost $100. To purchase a $140,000 rental property, closing costs for buyers are about $3,000 in Arizona. I also assumed the mortgage loan company required a 23% down payment, or $32,000.

**The 6% estimated appreciation rate is compounded.

***The 5% estimated increase in rental rates is based on United States Census Bureau Data. Cash flow is based on 100% occupancy. If the unit was vacant for one month out of each year, the 10-year cash-flow total would be $26,410 instead of $41,505. As such, the total gain would be $154,748 instead of $169,843.

****The 6% loan rate is based on a 30-year fixed, simple-interest loan. The original loan amount is $108,000 and amortization tables were used to calculate the interest and principal payments.

Since 1940, homes in the United States have increased in value at an average rate of 6 percent per year.[7] So after one year, her investment is now worth $8,400 more (6% x $140,000). That's $6,097 more than the $2,303 increase of the stock investor.

But her gains don't stop there.

The average national rental rate for a $140,000 unit is $1,300 per month.[8] The monthly mortgage payment for a $108,000 ($140,000 - $32,000 down payment) thirty-year fixed-interest mortgage at 6 percent interest is about $648.

According to industry standards, the average operating expenses for a single-family unit like this are about $377 a month.[9] This leaves a cash flow, or profit, of $275 per month ($1,300 in rent income – $648 mortgage payment – $377 a month in expenses = $275).

So the property investor's first year cash flow will be $3,300 ($275 x 12 months).

She has earned $11,700 so far ($8,400 in appreciation + $3,300 in cash flow).

But there's more.

The rent covers her mortgage payment, part of which goes to pay off the interest ($6,444) and part to the principal ($1,326). This creates equity.

Okay, now we can add it all up.

Her total net gain or profit in the first year is $13,026, nearly six times as much as the other stock investor, who earned $2,190.

Wow!

---

7 U.S. Census Bureau, retrieved 9/17/19 from https://fred.stlouisfed.org/series/MSPUS and from https://www.cnbc.com/2017/06/23/how-much-housing-prices-have-risen-since-1940.html/

8 Estimate obtained from Apartment List (August 28, 2019), retrieved 9/20/19 from https://www.apartmentlist.com/rentonomics/rental-data/

9 This includes property taxes, lawn care, insurance, and maintenance expenses. The estimate here excludes property management fees and salaries, because it assumes the property owner manages the property. Management fees and salaries comprise about one-third of operating costs, according to the National Apartment Association. The estimate here assumes that operating costs are 29% of the total gross income. For more details, see https://www.naahq.org/news-publications/units/september-2018/article/survey-operating-income-expenses-rental-apartment/

At the end of her first year, her total investment is now worth $45,026 ($32,000 down payment + $8,400 in appreciation + $3,300 in cash flow + $1,326 in principal equity), compared with $37,203 for the stock investor ($34,900 + $2,303).

But there's even more.

Because rent rates increase at a rate of about 5 percent a year, her rental payments can continue to increase through the years, offering her another hedge against inflation and additional profits.

Figure 2.1 summarizes everything I've just discussed.

At the end of the ten-year time period, the stock investor's total equity is $66,130 and the real estate investor's is $201,843 (a whopping ROI of 485 percent). The real estate investor's profit or gain is $169,843,[10] which is five times higher than the stock investor's gain of $31,230.

Figure 2.1 - Which Is Better: Stocks or Real Estate?

Ten-Year Comparison (Original Investment $35,000)

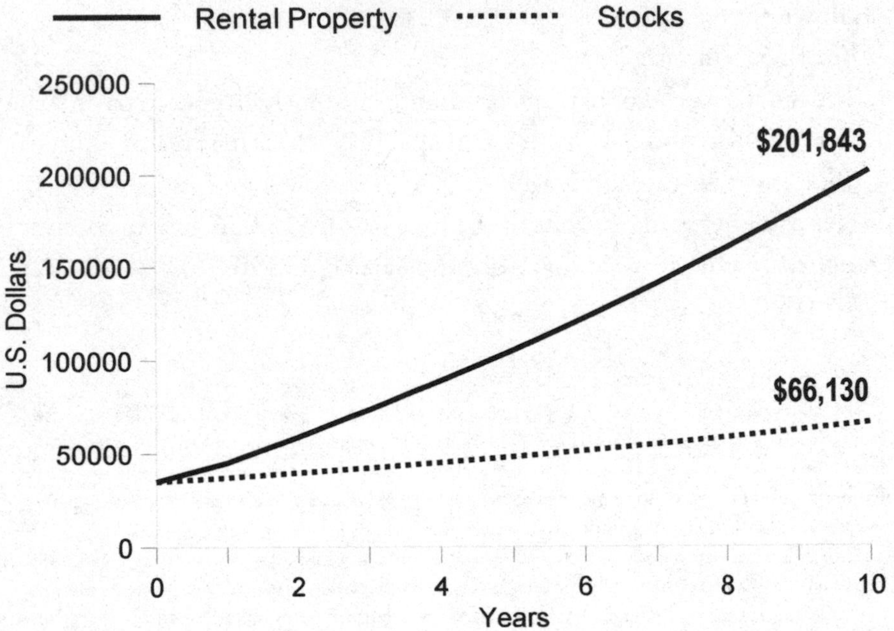

---

10 If the rental unit were vacant for one month out of every year, the total profit or gain would be $15,095 less, or $154,748.

So the bottom line is this: *If you owned just five to six small rental properties, you would generate $1 million in new assets in ten years.* Your total investments (including the money you put down to purchase the units) would be worth $1.2 million.

Have I convinced you that real estate is superior to the stock market?

If not, there's one more financial advantage of investing in real estate that I've left out of this comparison: *depreciation.* For a $140,000 property, a typical investor saves $600 to $1,400 a year on his or her taxes.

I'll elaborate on this and nine other financial advantages of investing in real estate in the next section. I'll follow that up with a list of four nonfinancial advantages and a final section that compares real estate to house flipping and stocks.

Ten Financial Reasons to Invest in Real Estate

1. Real Estate Has a Predictable Cash Flow

No matter where you live in the world, stock prices of companies and funds go up and down all the time, so it's difficult to predict how much money you'll make or lose on any particular day, month, or year.

Not so with real estate.

Except under extreme circumstances, like a disaster or a depression, revenue derived from real estate investments is very predictable every month. This helps you sleep at night.

Cash flow is the amount of money that flows into and out of your business over a set period of time, such as a month. A positive cash flow generally shows that a business is making a profit (after all operating expenses and mortgage payments have been made).

> **Definition #3**
>
> *Cash flow is the amount of money that flows into and out of your business.*

Many real estate rental investments around the world provide a 10 percent or better cash flow, compared to only 6.6 percent for the stock market, as I noted earlier.

But that's not all.

In addition to cash flow, your rent checks pay off the interest and principal on the mortgage every month and your property is appreciating in value.

2. Real Estate Appreciates in Value (Often Tax Free)

As noted in the example earlier in this chapter, homes in the United States are appreciating in value about 6 percent per year.

Since 1940, monthly apartment rental rates have appreciated about 5 percent a year, from $27 to $1,012.[11]

From 2000 to 2017, rent increased an average of 3.1 percent per year, compared with an average annual inflation rate of 2.1%.[12] This means that rent is increasing 48 percent faster than inflation [(3.1-2.1)/2.1=48%). Similar trends exist in other countries around the world.[13]

The appreciation in property values and rent means that you, as a real-estate investor, have a built-in hedge against inflation.[14]

Although the Dow Jones Industrial Average also has outperformed the inflation rate (6.6 percent from 1940 to 2017),[15] stocks lack cash flow and many other advantages discussed below.

3. Real Estate Can Be Leveraged

Why did the real estate investor do so much better in terms of return on investment than the stock market investor?

---

11 U.S. Census Bureau, retrieved 9/18.19 from https://www.census.gov/hhes/www/housing/census/historic/grossrents.html and from https://www.deptofnumbers.com/rent/us/

12 U.S. Bureau of Labor Statistics, retrieved 9/19/19 from http://www.in2013dollars.com/Rent-of-primary-residence/price-inflation and http://www.in2013dollars.com/Rent-of-primary- residence/price-inflation/2000-to-2017?amount=602/

13 "Global Cities House-price Index: Our Interactive Guide to Housing Data in the World's Most Desirable Cities," *The Economist* (March 11, 2019), retrieved 9/19/19 from https://www.economist.com/graphic-detail/2019/03/11/global-cities-house-price-index?date=2000-03&index=real_price&places=NYK&places=LON/

14 Some economists also argue that stock prices contain a hedge against inflation, because inflation is built into the increased prices for their goods and services. See Jeremy Siegel, "Stocks can be your best hedge against inflation," *Washington Post*, retrieved 9/25/19 from https://www.washingtonpost.com/business/stocks-can-be-your-best-hedge-against-inflation/ 2011/05/17/ AFj9tc8G_story.html/. But real estate investors have greater control over inflationary conditions, because they can increase their rent rates.

15 Macrotrends, retrieved 9/19/19 from https://www.macrotrends.net/1319/dow-jones-100-year- historical-chart/

In a word: *Leverage*.

Leverage is when you use *other people's money* (OPM) to make money.

The stock market investor earned 6.6 percent interest on the $34,900 he invested ($100 was spent on buying the stock).

Definition #4

Leverage means using other people's money (OPM) to make money

The real estate investor earned 6 percent equity from appreciation not only on the $32,000 she invested, but also 6 percent on the $108,000 she borrowed. Of course, she has to pay interest on the $108,000 she borrowed, *but that debt is covered by rent and* (get ready for another surprise) *the interest is tax deductible* (I'll talk about that in Chapter 10).

If you put 20 percent down to purchase a property and its value goes up 6 percent after one year (the average annual increase), you earned back more than one-fourth of your down payment. In three years, you'll have earned almost all of it back.

Definition #5

Equity is assets minus liabilities, and debt is a duty to pay someone.

If you obtain a fixed-interest mortgage rate, leverage also means that over time you're paying the mortgage off with cheaper dollars, because inflation almost always goes up, rarely down. This means you have another inflation hedge. And because rental rates tend to go up with inflation, your cash flow is also hedged.

In addition, as the rental income pays down the mortgage, you build equity (value) in a property, and that new equity can be leveraged for cash by either taking out a second loan or refinancing the entire loan. You can use this money to pay off your investors or buy another property—and, get this, you don't have to pay taxes on it, because it's equity, not income! (More on this in No. 6 below)

It is possible to leverage stock. It's called *margin trading*. You deposit a sum with your broker, who lends you money to purchase more stocks on credit.

You can make a lot of money in margin trading if the market goes up. But if it drops, you can lose a lot. In addition, you most likely will have to pay much higher interest rates on the loan than you would with a mortgage or even a higher-priced equity loan. Interest rates on property loans are less because the property becomes collateral for the loan. There is no collateral in margin trading, although your brokerage can call in the loan if the market takes a big dive, forcing you to pay the funds back immediately.

As you might expect, property values generally are much more stable than stock prices. However, during the 2008 to 2011 recession, both stocks and housing values in the United States and around the world dropped dramatically. That recession was caused in part by the deregulation of the financial industry, lax standards on lending, and excessive risk-taking.[16] Since then, the U.S. government has imposed safeguards to reduce the chances of another recession.

4. Real Estate Is Tax Deductible

When you earn a paycheck from a job, the government taxes the entire amount.

When you earn money through rental and commercial property, you're only taxed on the profit that is left after paying your expenses.

You can deduct the costs of maintenance, repairs, mortgage interest, taxes, and depreciation (see next section for more details on depreciation). In many cases, real estate investors pay little or no taxes year after year, even though they are building wealth through appreciation and principal payments.

5. Real Estate Is Depreciable

As things age, they tend to wear out and lose value.

In other words, they depreciate in value.

The wonderful thing about rental real estate is that the government lets you depreciate your property, which means you

Fact #3

Rental properties can be depreciated even though they usually increase in value.

---

16 Numerous factors are cited as causes and scholars and analysts sometimes disagree. A good summary can be found at Wikipedia, retrieved October 22, 2019, from https://en.wikipedia. org/wiki/ Financial_crisis_of_2007%E2%80%932008#Subprime_lending/

get to deduct a portion of its value and pay less in taxes each year. In fact, as noted above, many real estate investors pay no taxes at all.

Sound too good to be true?

Here's how it works.

Let's say you purchase a $140,000 rental property. The land is worth $28,000 and the building is worth $112,000.[17] For the next twenty-seven and a half years (that's how long until the government estimates it will take for the building to become worthless), the government allows you to deduct (depreciate) $4,072.72 from your income each year ($112,000 ÷ 27.5 = $4,072.72, or $339.39 each month) as long as you own the property.[18] (By the way, you can't depreciate the land because technically it doesn't "wear out.")

So let's say your cash flow (profit) from the property is $275 a month (or $3,300 for the year: $275 x 12). When tax time comes, you'll pay no taxes on the $3,300 you earned. In fact, your books will show a loss of $772.72 for the year ($4,072.72 - $3,300).

If your income is less than $100,000, you can deduct that $772.72 from other income you earn, which reduces your tax burden. If your income is between $100,000 and $150,000, you can only deduct a portion of the amount and you carry over the rest to the next tax year. If your income is above $150,000, you'll carry over all of the amount, unless real estate is your main profession—then you can deduct it all from any other income you earn.

The IRS allows real estate investors who earn less than $100,000 a year to deduct up to $25,000 in losses from real estate investments. Or you can elect to carry them over if you think your income will be higher in future years.

The odd thing about depreciation is that rental and commercial properties rarely lose value in the first hundred or so years of their existence. Values tend to increase over time, not decrease. So you, as an investor, get to take a deduction while your property increases in value.

---

17 As a rule, the ratio of land to improvements is 20-80. Some taxing jurisdictions don't separate the value of the two elements.

18 The actual amount of the depreciation in the first year is based on 11 rather than 12 months, so it is 1/12th less.

There's just one caveat.

To take full advantage of depreciation, you should not sell your property without purchasing another property of higher value. That's because the government will force you to pay a *depreciation recapture tax*, which means you're taxed on 25 percent of the depreciation you received since purchasing the property. One small consolation is that you get to pay it back in cheaper dollars, so the effective tax rate over a ten-year period is 21.2 percent, not 25 percent (assuming an inflation rate of 3 percent).

But one of the ways you can eliminate the depreciation recapture tax altogether is by selling your rental property and using the profits to purchase a more expensive rental property. In such a case, you pay nothing. This is called a *1031 Exchange*, which is discussed more under No. 8 below and in Chapter 12. The depreciation schedule starts again on the new property. This tax policy encourages investment in rental housing.

> ### Tip #3
>
> *A depreciation recapture tax on rental property can be eliminated if an investor invests the proceeds from a sale into a more expensive rental property.*

There are at least two other ways to avoid paying the recapture tax. You can bequeath your property to friends or loved ones. Or you can sell your property at a price lower than the depreciated value (not normally a good option, of course). You can also reduce your capital gains taxes by moving into the property and living there for at least two years before you sell (more on this later).

6. Real Estate Can Be Refinanced and You Pocket the Profit Tax Free

Let's say five years have passed and the rental property you purchased for $140,000 is now worth $187,352. This increase in value is based on a 6 percent average increase each year, compounded (see Table 2.1).

So now you have another $47,352 in equity (on top of the equity you've already earned through mortgage payments and the down payment). You can leave the equity in there or put it to work. Serious investors usually take the latter option. They take out a new mortgage or loan and use the equity to buy another rental property, pay off investors, or pay themselves.

The equity to pay yourself, by the way, is nontaxable, because it isn't income.

Can you now see why so many people become financially independent through real estate investing?

At this point, your head is probably swimming with dollar signs.

Put on your life vest.

It gets even better.

Because, when you eventually sell the property and take all of the profits (that is, you no longer reinvest the profits), you get

> **Fact #4**
>
> *Equity drawn from real estate is exempt from taxes.*

another tax advantage: you pay a lower tax rate than people who work for corporations or businesses.

7. Real Estate Profits Are Taxed at a Lower Tax Rate

Let's say after five years you decide to sell your rental property, which is now worth about $187,352. You're going to have to pay some income taxes, because the property is selling for more than you paid for it.

But don't cry (at least not for too long).

Because your profit is taxed as a *capital gain*, not as regular (earned) income.

And that means you usually will pay less taxes.

In the United States, the capital gain tax brackets for single people are 0 percent for gains below $40,000 ($80,000 for married couples); 15 percent for gains between $40,001 and $441,450 ($80,001 to $496,600 for couples); and 20 percent for gains that exceeds $441,451 ($496,601 for couples). In contrast, earned income above $40,126 is taxed at rates between 22 percent and 37 percent.

For example, let's say you earn $40,000 from a job and a $100,000 profit on the sale of a property, for a total income of $140,000. In terms of your job income (the $40,000), IRS rules require you to pay 10 percent of the amount up to $9,875 and 12 percent on the amount from $9,876 to $40,125. In other words, you'll pay $4,603 ($988 plus $3,615) in federal taxes on your $40,000 salary.

On the sale of your property you'll pay 15 percent, which is $15,000 (15% x $100,000 = $15,000). So your total tax bill for the year will be $19,603.

Another person who earns $140,000 from a "normal" job will pay $988 (10 percent on first $9,875), plus $3,630 (12 percent on the income up to $40,125); plus $9,988 (22 percent on the income up to $85,525), plus $13,074 (24 percent on the income up to $140,000)—for a total tax bill of $27,680.

You "save" $8,077.

In short, your effective tax rate is 14 percent ($19,603 ÷ $140,000) and their tax rate is 20 percent ($27,680 ÷ $140,000).

This is another reason the rich get richer. They earn much or most of their income through investments that are taxed as capital gains, not income.

This might seem unfair, but it's the law (it's designed, by the way, to encourage investment), and there's no reason why you, a first-time investor, shouldn't take advantage of capital gains tax rates, too.

> **Fact #5**
>
> *The rich get richer because much of their income is taxed as a capital gain, not as regular income.*

8. Real Estate Gains Are Deferrable

But let's say after selling your property you don't want to take the profit.

You want to reinvest in another property, because you haven't reached your financial goals yet.

If you purchase a more expensive real estate property, you can wipe out the depreciation recapture tax on the previous property (see No. 5 above) and you don't have to pay capital gains taxes on the profit from the sale of the property.

Reinvesting profits to "defer recognition of capital gains" is known as a *1031 Exchange* (the name comes from Section 1031 of the United States Internal Revenue Code; many other countries have similar laws).

A 1031 Exchange allows you to use your money, tax free, to continue investing.

That's why so many real estate moguls pay so little in taxes.

You only pay when you no longer reinvest the profits.

I'll give you more details about a 1031 Exchange in Chapter 11.

> **Tip #4**
>
> *A 1031 Exchange allows you to cut depreciation, recapture taxes, and defer capital gains taxes.*

9. Real Estate Is Improvable (Sweat Equity)

Because real estate is tangible, you can build equity by fixing up the property.

Do-it-yourselfers love this advantage.

They purchase a property, fix it up, and the equity increases far more than the actual costs of fixing it up. This is called "sweat equity," which means you aren't taxed for your work.

Of course, you can hire others to do the work. But you want to make sure the improvements bring more cash in than you pay out.

10. Real Estate Offers Asset Protection

So I'm guessing that, if you're still reading at this point, you're very interested in investing in rental properties.

But in the back of your mind, you've still got some doubts: "What if things go wrong? What if the market takes a dive, like it did in 2008? What if a natural disaster hits? What if my place burns down?"

Real estate, unlike stocks, offers asset protection, not just for the property but for your personal assets as well. In contrast, if the company in which you own stock has a bad year, you're out of luck.

Real estate is one of the few investments that can be insured. Although insurance is an expense, the cost is covered by the property's income and it's tax deductible. You have peace of mind knowing that if the real property is destroyed, your loss is covered.

Another legal advantage of real estate is that it can be placed into a limited liability company, or LLC (see Chapter 4). This organizational form allows you to protect your personal wealth by individuating and protecting your assets. If, for any reason, your business is sued, your other personal assets, like your house, bank accounts, and investments, are protected because they aren't part of your LLC.

Every property you buy should be placed into its own individual LLC. That's how you protect your wealth.

Imagine, for instance, that one of your tenants falls in the shower and is injured. If all of your properties were under a single entity, that resident would have the legal right to pursue damages based on the entire asset value of all your investments in that entity. If, however, each property is its own LLC, that resident normally will only be able to seek damages from that entity. Your other holdings would be unaffected.

In short, the risks associated with investing in real estate are far, far less than those you take with stocks and many other investment options.

Four Nonfinancial Reasons to Invest in Real Estate

The ten financial reasons to invest in real estate wouldn't be very helpful to investors if they couldn't find the time to invest or if they needed lots of formal education. Fortunately, neither of these is a prerequisite. Here are four nonfinancial reasons that make real estate a great investment.

1. You Don't Have to Quit Your Job

You can search for new properties to buy or fix up in your spare time and on your days off. You can keep working your regular job until you become financially free.

2. You Don't Need a Formal Education

You don't need a college degree or a real estate license to invest in real estate. You don't even need a lot of knowledge about real estate or be an advanced negotiator.

If you have good credit and a steady income, you most likely can purchase or invest in real estate right now (whether it's a primary home or a rental property).

> **Fact #6**
>
> *Two advantages of investing in real estate: You don't have to quit your job and you don't have to be an expert investor.*

Of course, the more you learn the better equipped you'll be to make good decisions. I'm a big proponent of self-education, not just in the field of real estate but also personal development (topics we'll discuss later).

3. You Don't Need a Lot of Money to Invest

Many people think you need a lot of money for the down payment in order to get a loan.

If you purchase a rental property, you normally will have to put something down. Most banks and mortgage companies require 20 to 25 percent, which helps protect them should you default on the loan.

That may seem like a lot, but consider the fact that you only have to put down one out of every four or five dollars. The bank or mortgage company gives you the rest.

Now that's leverage.

If you can't afford the entire down payment, there are other options. You can find partners or investors, both of whom may be friends or family members. You might not even have to put any of your own money down. We'll explore financing in Chapter 5.

> **Myth #2**
>
> *You have to be wealthy to invest in real estate.*

The more properties you buy and manage properly, the easier it is to get investment funds. Eventually, banks and mortgage companies will loan the money to your company rather than you.

Today I put only a small amount of my own money into purchasing rental properties, so I can invest in more deals. Investors provide most of the money. And I pay them a good return on their investment. That's why they keep coming back.

4. As Your Business Grows, You Can Work Less

Today I spend very little time directly managing my properties. I pay others to collect the rents, maintain the property, do the books, and deal with renter problems. I focus on bigger issues, such as how economic trends will affect my business and how to find good deals.

As your income increases, you'll have the resources to hire others to help you out, which frees you up to do the things you want to do.

To achieve financial freedom, usually the best plan is to continue selling and buying up properties and deferring capital gains and depreciation taxes until you have the cash flow you need. After that, you can buy that beach house in Malibu and declare, as actor Jackie Gleason used to say, "How sweet it is."

> **Myth #3**
>
> *You don't always have to put money down to purchase property.*

Advantages of Real Estate Rental Investment vs. Fix & Flip

During the last two decades, the popularity of "fixing and flipping" homes has soared in part because of television shows touting the high profits that one can make.

I've met many people who have had success doing this.

There isn't enough statistical data available to compare real estate rental investment practices to fix-and-flip practices. But my experience is that, in the long run, buying rental properties offers much higher profits (and lower taxes) and is far less risky than fixing and flipping. It also is a lot less work.

Table 2.2 provides a summary of the advantages between real estate investing versus fixing and flipping. I've also included stocks in the table, a topic already thoroughly addressed in this chapter.

Items 1 through 10 show the advantages of real estate over stocks and flipping.

Items 11 and 12 show little or no differences between the three business models.

Items 13 through 15 show the advantages of stocks over real estate.

And item 16 shows the advantage of fix & flip over stocks and real estate.

Let's start with No. 1 and work our way down.

Table 2.2

Summary of Advantages of Real Estate vs. Fix & Flip and Stocks

Advantage	Real Estate	Stocks	Fix & Flip
1. Long-Term Return on Investment	High	Low	See text
2. Leveraging Other People's Money at Low Interest Rates	High	Low	Moderate
3. Hedge Against Inflation*	High	Moderate	Low
4. Predictable Cash Flow	Yes	No	No
5. Build Equity through Mortgage Payments	Yes	No	No
6. Can be Depreciated	Yes	No	No
7. Defer Capital Gains via 1031 Exchange	Yes	No	No
8. Profits Can be Distributed through Equity/Refinance Loans	Yes	No	No
9. Amount of Risk**	Low	Moderate	High
10. Possible to Create "Sweat Equity"	Yes	No	Yes
11. Losses Are Tax Deductible***	Yes	Yes, but	Yes
12. Lower Tax Rates via Capital Gains****	Yes	Yes	Depends
13. Easy to Sell	No	Yes	No
14. Easy to Purchase	No	Yes	No
15. Easy to Maintain/Amount of Labor Needed	Moderate	Low	High
16. Short-Term Return on Investment	Moderate	Low	High

*In the short term, stocks are not a good hedge against inflation. But they are a good hedge in the long term. See Jeremy Siegel, "Stocks can be your best hedge against inflation,"*Washington Post,* retrieved 9/25/19 from https://www.washingtonpost.com/business/stocks-can-be-your-best- hedge-against-inflation/ 2011/05/17/ AFj9tc8G_story.html/

**All three types of investors can protect their personal property by investing through LLCs. However, real estate investors can purchase insurance to protect their investment against catastrophic loss, such as storm damage. There is no insurance for stock investments.

***Stock investors must generate gains to deduct losses, with the exception of $1,500 per year (or $3,000 per couple). Losses in excess of these amounts are carried to future years. Investors who qualify as real estate professionals may deduct all losses from other income; nonprofessionals whose incomes are greater than $150,000 must carry over losses; those under $100,000 can deduct up to $25,000, and the amount diminishes as income moves from $100,000 to $150,000. Source: Charles Schwab, retrieved 9/25/19 from https://www.schwab.com/public/schwab/investing/ retirement_and_planning/taxes/resources/ tax-deductible-investment-expenses/

****The flipper would qualify for capital gains tax rate if he held onto the property for one year before selling.

1. As I discussed earlier, ***the historical return*** on real estate rental property far outstrips stocks (Item 1). Using data from the 1940s to the present, a typical real estate property generates a profit that is five times greater over a ten-year period (485 percent v. 89 percent ROI). Stocks produce a decent average annual yield of 6.6 percent, *but real estate produces an average return of 19.2 percent!*

Fixing and flipping homes (F&F) also can offer moderate-to-high returns in the long run if the flipper is constantly buying and fixing up homes. A general rule is that a flipper will spend—on purchasing and fixing up the house—no more than 70 percent of its final selling price. So if it costs $20,000 to fix up a home and the flipper wants to sell it at $140,000, she would pay no more than $78,000 for the home ([$78,000 + $20,000] ÷ $140,000 = 70%).

This is a great model, but finding good buys can be difficult.

Phoenix, for example, was a prime market for F&F after the 2008 housing meltdown and recession. Thousands of homes were sold at low prices, fixed, and flipped. Today, however, housing prices have recovered and there is a lot more competition for homes, which makes it difficult to find good buys.

So I've rated the long-term ROI for F&F at "moderate"—somewhere between real estate rentals and stocks.

2. All three forms of investment can ***leverage other people's money*** (Item 2). But real estate rentals can do so at much lower interest rates than flippers and stock investors, because real estate investors can finance their home purchases over thirty years.

Flippers often turn to *hard money lenders*—privately-owned companies that loan money for short periods of time—to purchase and fix up a home. The goal is to fix and sell the home as quickly as possible, because even though hard money lenders usually don't charge fees or closing costs, the interest rates on their loans can be very high (16 percent or more). If the flipper fails to pay the loan back in a predetermined amount of time, the lender can foreclose on the house, and the flipper loses everything.

3. Real estate rentals offer a big *hedge against inflation*, through appreciation, rent increases (Item 3), and mortgage paydown.[19] Holding onto stocks for a long time also can be a hedge against inflation, because companies raise the prices of their goods or services in response to inflationary pressures. Flippers usually turn their properties around quickly, so they don't offer much of a hedge against inflation.

4. Real estate rentals offer a *predictable cash flow* because rent money comes in every month and the costs of maintaining the property are fairly predictable (Item 4). Stock prices can change without notice, and flippers may have to sell their properties for less than they desire when the deadline for repaying the hard money loans comes due.

5-8. Real estate rentals offer four other advantages that neither stocks nor F&F properties offer: *equity through mortgage payments* (Item 5), *depreciation* (Item 6), *deferred capital gains via 1031 Exchange* (Item 7), and *profits can be distributed through equity or refinance loans on the property*, which means the money is not taxed (Item 8).

9. The *amount of risk* is lowest in real estate (Item 9), because there is no immediate deadline to repay loans and because home prices tend to be much more stable than stock prices.

10. Real estate rentals and F&F can both benefit from *sweat equity* (Item 10). Stocks don't.

11. Losses from all three forms of investment are *tax deductible* (Item 11), but real estate professionals and professional house flippers (called dealer-traders) can deduct losses from other income in the year they occur. Part-time real estate rental investors can take full deductions if their income is less than $100,000 a year.

12. All three forms of investing can benefit from *capital gains* taxes (Item 12), which usually are lower than tax rates for ordinary income. However, the property or stock investor can only take advantage of capital gains if the investment is held for at least one year. This is particularly

---

19 Fixed-rate mortgages are hedges against inflation, because as time passes and inflation makes dollars less valuable, you're paying your loan back with "cheaper" dollars.

difficult for house flippers, because the cost of hard money loans often will negate any tax advantage. Profits earned in less than one year are treated as ordinary income, which means tax rates as high as 37 percent, compared with capital gains tax rates of 20 percent (and 15 percent for those whose income is under $434,550 a year).

13-14. Without doubt, stocks are *easier to purchase and sell* than real estate (Items 13 and 14)—or, as business people say, stocks have more *liquidity* than real estate. All you need to do is establish an account with a brokerage firm (online accounts are easy to set up), put some money into the account, and click a few buttons to purchase a stock or a fund.

15. Of course, stocks also are much *easier to maintain* than real estate investments (Item 15). Flipping requires a lot of labor or labor costs. Rental properties must also be maintained, but labor costs are spread out over a longer period of time. Most rental property investors will do major improvements to their properties only after they buy and/or before they sell.

16. Flipping houses has one clear advantage over the other investments: a faster route to profits *(short-term returns on investment) (Item 16)*. A flipper can earn tens of thousands of dollars in several months buying and flipping houses. The gains in stocks and real estate generally take more time.

To illustrate, let's take a house that a flipper has just sold for $140,000.

Using the 70 percent rule, she paid $78,000 for the house and put $20,000 in improvements.

Her closing costs include escrow fees to the title company ($500), a title insurance policy ($1,000), recording fees ($50), a home warranty (the seller paid half the costs of a policy, $250), taxes ($500) and real estate fees and commissions ($7,000).

Her costs of borrowing $98,000 in hard money at 12 percent interest for six months—which gives her time to buy, fix, and sell the property— is $3,500.

The flipper's total costs are now at $110,800.

Subtracting that amount from the selling price gives the flipper a profit of $29,200.

Let's say the flipper is able to fix and flip two houses a year, using only her sweat equity.

That would give her a yearly income of $58,400.

Using 2019 tax rates, the IRS would take 10 percent on income up to $13,600, 12 percent on income up to $51,800, and 22 percent on income over $51,800. So her total tax bill would be $8,808, and her net income would be $49,592. Eighteen percent of her income would go to taxes.

By comparison, if a real estate rental property investor purchased two homes, each worth $140,000, he would have earned through appreciation, cash flow, and principal payments more than $26,000 at the end of the year (see Table 2.1). The real estate investor pays no taxes, however, because of deductions from interest payments, maintenance, and depreciation.

So flipping is more profitable in the short term.

But flipping is a LOT more work.

The rental property investor puts in a lot less labor yet produces more than half of the income of the flipper. In addition, the investor doesn't have to worry about buying and fixing up more homes next year. The rental property investor would earn more than $26,000 in the next year and every year thereafter. The only thing he has to do is keep the property up.

Chapter Three

You've Got What It Takes

Not everyone makes a good real estate investor or landlord. People who are afraid of hard work or taking risks are not well suited to the profession.

But real estate investing isn't rocket science.

As I pointed out in the first chapter, you only need three traits to be financially independent through real estate:

> *(1) the motivation to succeed,*
> *(2) a good work ethic, and*
> *(3) the willingness to educate yourself about real estate and learn from your mistakes.*

This chapter elaborates on the first two, drawing partly on my own experiences.

The third trait is examined in the chapters that follow. I'll show you, in ten steps, how to set up an LLC, get your investment money, find your ideal market and property, manage your property, do your books, and file your taxes.

Motivation, Hard Work, and Lead Dogs

Real estate investors often ask me how I got my start in real estate.

They want to know my secrets to success.

The truth of the matter is that success is usually a complicated process. It doesn't begin with the first property purchase. It begins with some fundamental values, often acquired during a person's childhood, and some clearly-defined goals.

Or at least that's how I see it.

I was born in Everett, Washington, in the early 1960s—a time of relatively low unemployment, low inflation, and appreciating property values (ideal for investing, by the way).

My father was a sheet metal worker and an honest man who was loyal to friends and family. He was responsible, and never job-hopped.

He eventually launched a successful air conditioning and heating repair business.

My mother was a hairdresser who worked out of our home. A loving woman, she developed a loyal following of customers.

My parents worked hard all of their lives. I respect them for that.

They provided for me and my two siblings. We never went hungry and always had a roof over our heads.

But my parents never had a lot of extra money.

They never achieved *financial freedom*.

My father worked until he died in his late eighties.

Dad never gave me much guidance when it came to money.

But he did say one thing that has stuck in my head all these years.

"If you aren't the lead dog, the scenery never changes." (Dad, by the way, borrowed this saying from Lewis Grizzard, a famous twentieth-century newspaper editor and writer.)

All my business life, I've never felt the need to be the top dog.

I like to work with others as equals. That's what teamwork is all about.

But I certainly never wanted to be the dog at the back of the pack.

The path to financial freedom requires you to take the lead—to be motivated; to be your own boss.

> **Tip #5**
>
> *To be financially free, you need to be a lead dog and educate yourself.*

Not everyone is good at this.

Some people actually prefer to work for others. They like to please others or be told what to do. Some aren't comfortable making a lot of tough decisions.

Others don't like working for bosses but do so because they need a steady job to feel secure. They are afraid to try something else.

Some simply don't want to work hard. They place greater importance on other things in life, such as hobbies or sports or raising children.

And, of course, there are some people who are simply lazy and don't want to work. (Ever notice how they tend to be the topic of conversation at family get-togethers?)

There is absolutely nothing wrong with not wanting to be your own boss.

After all, being in charge means a lot of responsibility and sometimes a lot of stress.

Being your own boss also means that when problems arise, you often have to drop everything to solve them. No one else is going to fix things.

But people who work for themselves also have a big, big advantage over other people: The fruits of their labors go directly to them, not others!

Being a lead dog means you need to actively seek out information about real estate.

Reading this book is a first step.

Read others when you can.

And don't be afraid to seek out the advice of knowledgeable people, especially real estate

> **Tip #6**
>
> *Read books about real estate investing and seek the advice of knowledgeable people.*

agents, accountants, attorneys, property managers, appraisers, contractors, and other investors.

You'll find that most people love to give advice. Everyone wants to feel valued, and there is nothing more flattering than being asked to share your knowledge or opinion on a topic.

If you, in turn, share with them, you'll earn their trust and begin building life-long alliances and friendships.[20] Chapter 13 offers more tips on education.

Once you decide you're a good candidate to purchase a property, your next step is to set some goals.

You Need Goals

As I've written in other places, having a goal or goals is not optional.

You must have them.

Goals help you focus.

They make you decisive.

And ultimately, goals contribute to your success.

I highly recommend you write your goals down.

I didn't do that when I first started out. I knew I wanted to be my own boss someday, but I never formally verbalized or recorded it. I started my own real estate management and investing business nine years after working for a real estate investor (who went on to build a real-estate empire).

Today, I write my goals down because they keep me focused and decisive.

When I make decisions, I ask myself, "Will this decision help me achieve my goals?"

If the answer is no, then I move on to other matters.

Only by staying focused on your goals will you be able to achieve them.

---

20 There is another category of people who want to purchase a rental property: Those who have cash assets but don't have enough time. Don't purchase a rental property if you don't have the time to maintain the property and your business. Instead, I suggest you invest in a private company that buys apartments or commercial properties. I'm not talking about real estate stock funds. Those typically do not produce returns any greater than the stock market. I'm talking about companies, like mine, that need capital to purchase or build apartment communities. The rates of return on these investments can be 7% or more plus part ownership in a community. To qualify, you usually have to invest a substantial sum of money ($50,000 or more) and in some cases have to be an accredited investor (I discuss this in Chapter 5). Be sure to research the companies and projects they are offering, as there are scams out there.

What Is a Goal?

A goal is something you plan to achieve.

A goal should contain an action of some sort and a time frame.

For example, if you're new to the real estate business, your goal might be simple, such as "I want to purchase a rental property within one year and rent it." The property could be a condominium, a house, or a small apartment complex.

This is a reasonable and measurable goal.

It includes an action (purchasing a property) *and a time frame* (one year).

Your decisions (or at least some of them) during the next year should be focused on achieving that goal. Then, at the end of the year, you can assess whether you achieved that goal and, if not, why not. At that point, you may wish to change or modify your goals.

> **Definition #6**
>
> *A goal is something you plan to achieve.*

Goal-setting is not a static process. You'll be constantly creating, modifying, and achieving (or rejecting) goals.

Because you're reading this book, I'm assuming you also have the goal of wanting to be financially free someday.

The first step here is to define what you mean by "financially free." For many people it means "being your own boss and living comfortably on the money your real estate investments bring in."

Let's get just a little more specific: How much money do you need to be financially free?

If your current job produces a salary that is sufficient, including health insurance, then you might use that to set your goal. Once you can generate the same amount of income from real estate as you do from your salary, you can quit your job. If you need more than your current salary, then estimate best as you can.

So let's say, for illustrative purposes, that you and/or your family need $50,000 a year to be comfortable. That's not a lot of money, but if you could earn that much being your own boss, you conclude that would be a good life.

So, to sum up, to achieve your goal of being financially free, you need to earn $50,000 a year from your real estate investments.

Does that sound daunting?

It's not as difficult as it may seem.

If you own a rental property that is producing a $275 a month in positive cash flow after all bills are paid, that property produces a $3,300 positive cash flow (or profit). Here's the math:

$275 per month cash flow X 12 months = $3,300 cash flow per year

So the next question is this: How many rental properties would you need to purchase and lease to achieve your goal of $50,000 a year?

The answer is fifteen. Here's the math: $50,000 ÷ $3,300 = 15.2

So you would have to purchase fifteen rental properties.

Now that sounds like a lot, and it is for someone with little cash on hand.

But remember, a rental property normally will increase in value over time and you're building equity with each mortgage payment. If you look at Table 2.1 in the second chapter, you'll see that after only three years, your property will have $54,228 in equity—equity that you can borrow to purchase your next property.

And when you own several rental properties and have some experience under your belt, other opportunities will come your way. You may, for example, decide to sell a couple of rental properties and reinvest the equity in a four- or eight-unit apartment dwelling, which generally provides a stronger cash flow than single-family units.

Assuming you can buy one rental unit every year or two, five to ten years then becomes a reasonable time line for achieving your goal of becoming financially free. Or, alternatively, if you're a person of patience and just want to have a couple of rentals, you can easily attain $1 million in gross revenues in less than twenty years. That might sound like a long time, but if you're in your twenties or thirties now, that means you could "retire" in your forties or fifties.

Who could complain about that? You retire a decade or two earlier than 90 percent of the population.

On the other hand, if you make good decisions, chances are the time to your goal will shrink. A four-unit apartment complex, for example, could produce $20,000 a year in cash flow, and it wouldn't cost as much as buying four separate single-family home rental properties. You benefit from what economists call *economies of scale* (shared walls and a roof line reduces per unit costs).

As the conditions and your personal interests change, you'll modify, eliminate, or create new goals.

Nothing wrong with that.

The purpose of a goal is not to force you into a particular course of action, but to keep you focused and decisive. It's okay to change your goals. Mine change often.

> **Tip #7**
>
> *Goals can and should change as conditions change.*

In fact, after I made my first property purchase, I altered my goals.

Goals and My First Step to Financial Freedom

My first investment was a two-bedroom condominium.

I rented it out to people who wanted to come to Phoenix for a short vacation or weekend getaway.

I purchased it for $116,000. I put $16,000 down and financed the rest.

That was a lot of money for me back then.

But I knew I would get it back.

When I sold the condo seven years later, I reaped a $70,000 profit.

The only downside was that I had to pay capital gains taxes on the profit.

Then I learned I could purchase an apartment property without putting anything down.

You read that right: *nothing.*

A few years later, a partner and I purchased a 182-unit apartment community in Sun City, Arizona, for $9 million.

We didn't put a cent down of our own money. Everything came from investors. (I'll show you how to do that in Chapter 5.)

My partner and I still own that property, which is now valued at $25 million.

Even though my partner and I were experienced property investors at that time, that wasn't the reason investors jumped on the wagon.

> **Myth #4**
>
> *You need to spend your own money to buy apartments and commercial property.*

It was our business plan.

We put together a strong proposal which clearly showed investors how much money the apartment community would make and how much they would get in return. A sound business plan is a requisite for getting into the bigger deals (see Chapter 5).

We paid our investors off in five years.

Some of them still invest in projects we are doing today.

The moral of this story is that goals can change. Although I made money on the condo, I decided that apartments were a more profitable investment and, best of all, I could purchase them with the help of other people's money.

John's Goals

When my acquaintance John told me that he was interested in purchasing a rental property, I knew he was a good candidate because he had the time (he was semi-retired), was pretty good at fixing things, and was motivated (not just for himself, but for his daughter, too).

He had never invested in a rental property.

But after reading some of my books, he told me, "I should have gotten into real estate thirty years ago. Better late than never."

John decided to purchase either a condominium or a small home.

Although his social security income and part-time work provided a comfortable living, he figured a day would come when he would quit working, and a little extra cash flow would enable him to do that and still be comfortable. He also wanted to build equity in the property so he could leave the business to his lovely college-aged daughter. These were John's long-term goals.

His short-term goal was to purchase a condominium or home within six months and rent it on a twelve-month lease. He changed this goal, however, when the seller gave him thousands of dollars in free furniture. He decided to rent the unit on a seasonal or short-term basis, which allowed him to charge more rent.

What Else Do You Need to Invest in Real Estate?

As implied in previous discussions, a good credit history is helpful but not necessary.

Banks and investors are less likely to lend money to people who have defaulted on previous loans or who fail to pay their bills.

So if your credit rating isn't quite up to par, make that a top priority.

Pay your bills on time.

Build your credit.

In the meantime, spend your time learning all you can about investing in real estate. When your credit rating pops back up, you'll be ready to move.

Take Action Now

Before leaving this chapter, I want to emphasize that you should act as quickly as you can if you want to be financially independent.

Time is precious.

> **Tip #8**
>
> *Financial freedom often can be achieved in a decade or so.*

No one knows that better than John, who turned sixty-five the year he purchased his first rental property.

The plan I lay out in this book roughly estimates that the typical person taking a modest course of real estate investing can achieve some level of independence in five years and certainly full independence in twenty years.

The length of time will depend upon how much wealth you need, the decisions you make, and market conditions.

There are no guarantees in life.

But over the decades I've helped hundreds of people achieve financial freedom through real estate, including John, who said he would have acted sooner had he read my books earlier. He nevertheless is grateful that he learned it now rather than later, and he believes he can achieve his modest long-term goal within five years.

Part II

How to Find, Purchase, and Maintain a Rental Property

Chapter Four

Step 1: Set Up Your Business

I f you're still reading this book, I'll assume you want to continue on a path toward financial freedom.

> That's great news!
> So what's the next step?
> You need to create your own company.
> That's what John did.
> He created a Limited Liability Company.[21]

Why Create an LLC?

John didn't need to create an LLC to purchase or manage a rental property.

He could have used his own name. This is known as a *sole proprietorship*—a company run by one individual with no distinction between the business and him. He would get all profits and would be responsible for all the debts, losses, and liabilities.

Lots of people who want to buy and rent property use their own names.

But I don't recommend this option, because if you or one of your rental properties suffer a catastrophic financial loss (not likely but possible), your creditors will go after not only your business assets but your personal assets

---

21 The IRS recognized the LLC in 1988 and by the late 1990s every state in the union recognized the business entity. Kathryn Kobe, *Small Business GDP: Update 2002-2010* Small Business Administration (January 2012), a report prepared under contract no. SBAHQ-10-M-0258.

as well, which includes money you have in the bank, your home, car, and other possessions.

To provide some protection for his personal assets, John created an LLC and put his daughter's name on the business as well. One person can own an LLC or it can have multiple members. In additional to protecting personal assets, an LLC has two advantages over traditional corporations:

> **Fact #7**
>
> *A Limited Liability Company (LLC) protects your personal assets.*

(1) LLCs are not double taxed. Profits of regular C corporations are taxed at the corporate level and then again when the profits are distributed to individual shareholders, who have to pay on their personal tax returns. LLCs are only taxed once. The profits "pass through" the business into the hands of the manager-member or the members. They are responsible for paying federal and state taxes, if any.

(2) LLCs allow all members to control the company. Shareholders rarely control a large corporation, which usually is under the authority of the board of directors and management. As you might expect, those who control a corporation don't always act in the best interests of the shareholders.

How to Create an LLC

There are two ways to create an LLC.

The first is to do it yourself. The second is to hire a professional.

Let me talk about hiring others first.

If you have the financial resources, I recommend you hire a professional, like an attorney or an accountant, to set up your LLC. My colleague and friend Robert Kiyosaki, author of *Rich Dad Poor Dad*, emphasizes the importance of creating a team for your business. Attorneys and accountants can save you a lot of money and ensure that you do not fall into legal trouble.

But many of you are just getting started and don't have the resources to hire professionals. Filing the paperwork to create an LLC is not complicated. But keep in mind that as your company grows, you will need to create a team of experts to help you, because everything becomes more complicated as your business grows.

You begin the process of creating an LLC by creating a name for your business (like John Properties LLC), and then you file an application with your state. Your business name needs to be unique. You don't want people to confuse your business with other businesses. And if you pick a name that creates confusion, the other business may sue and prevent you from using the name.

All fifty states and free-market countries around the world offer limited liability forms of business. But not all allow one person to form and own an LLC, as does the United States. Some states regulate LLCs through the secretary of state's office, while others have a corporation commission or a commerce department. All states require a fee to create the LLC (from $40 in Kentucky to $500 in Massachusetts). Most also require an annual fee (California's fee is highest at $800 a year; Arizona and seven other states have no annual fee).

To register your business name, simply go online and type in a search bar: "Create an LLC in (fill in your state's name)."

Websites will pop up.

Ignore the "dot com" websites.

They want you to file the name through them so they can make a profit.

Don't do that.

Look for the **.gov** listing. The cost is less if you file directly with your state.

In Arizona, for example, it costs $50 to file "Articles of Organization" for an LLC (but don't worry, the articles are created for you). By comparison, a leading **.com** site wanted $99 to file the articles.

Each state has a different set of rules for completing LLC applications.

But here are some of the basic steps.

> ## Tip #9
> *You don't have to pay someone to set up your LLC, but hire an attorney if you have questions about complying with the law.*

1. Choose a Name

Pick a name that represents the image you want to project to the world. Avoid cutesy or unusual names. You want to project an air of professionalism to the community.

When you apply for the LLC, most sites will allow you to search their records to see if that name is already taken in your state. If so, you can change the spelling or add another word to the title to make it different.

2. Choose a Statutory (or Registered) Agent

The statutory/registered agent is your point of contact with the state and the public.

You can do it yourself or you can hire a company to perform the job.

If you use your own address, be cautious. Some states require the address to be open from nine to five to accept service of process (a notice of a lawsuit). If you travel or are not home, the plaintiff (the person who filed the lawsuit) can go back to court and tell the judge they couldn't serve you. In that case, a default judgment is issued, which means you lose the case. So if your state requires someone to be available on a regular basis, your best option is probably paying a company a fee (often about $125 a year) to serve as your registered agent.[22]

3. File the Articles of Organization

This is easy.

You just need to tell the state whether the LLC will be member-managed or manager-managed. The former means that some or all members of the LLC will manage the business. The latter means that one or more members (or even a non-member) will manage and the others will be passive owners.

If you're filing a one-member LLC (meaning you alone are the owner of the business), then choose the manager-member option. The state will produce and send you the Articles of Organization after you pay.

---

22 If you use Wyoming, Nevada or Delaware LLC for their asset protection benefits, but you don't live in one of those states, you'll have to hire a registered agent in that state.

Every LLC, including single-member LLCs, should have an *operating agreement.*[23] Like the bylaws for a corporation, an operating agreement is a road map for how the LLC will operate.

Setting up your business can be more complicated if you have one or more partners.

In such a case, you should always create an operating agreement. This ensures all business owners understand how the LLC is going to be operated and managed. The operating agreement should reduce future conflict.

You also may want to create a website for your business. Some states allow you to select the URL (Uniform Resource Locator), which is the address of a World Wide Web page. Be sure that address is available before you file your business name.

If you're unsure about any of the steps provided above, I advise you to seek the advice of a business attorney.

Some states will charge an extra fee for "expedited delivery" of your LLC paperwork. Unless you need them immediately, don't pay the extra fee. Use it to buy an inexpensive bookkeeping software program (see Chapter 9).

4. Register with Local Governments

Some cities and jurisdictions require you to register your business with them as well. Some of them impose a small tax on business organizations. Check with your local government if you need to file with them.

5. Obtain an Employee Identification Number

For tax purposes, you must use your own social security number if you operate as a sole proprietorship. If you create an LLC, you will need an *Employer Identification Number* (EIN), because you will need to create a separate business checking account.

When you bill customers (excluding renters), many will ask you to fill out an IRS W-9 form (easy to complete), which enables them, at the end of the year, to send you a 1099 tax form (income from sources other than a regular job) showing how much they paid you. (Uncle Sam wants to make sure your customer isn't fabricating expenses and that you're reporting all

---

23 In Texas the OA is called a Company Agreement.

of your income. But don't worry, you probably won't have to pay any taxes because of depreciation and maintenance costs.)

The IRS issues the EIN free of charge online. Just search, "Apply for EIN," or follow this link (https://www.irs.gov/businesses/small-businesses-self-employed/apply-for-an-employer-identification-number-ein-online).

Once again, watch out for imposters—they use all kinds of gimmicks to trick you into thinking you're on the **.gov** site. Some even charge $50 for an EIN.

6. Open a Business Checking Account and Order Some Business Cards

You'll need a bank account to run your business.

The bank or credit union will require you to provide a driver's license (or passport), LLC paperwork (provided by the state), tax identification number (if applicable), and social security number. The law requires these institutions to obtain this information.

For an initial deposit, ideally you should write a check from your personal account and make it out to your LLC. If you deposit large sums of money, the financial officer may require you to document the source of the funds. Financial institutions are required to report money laundering or other suspicious activity.

I also recommend you order some business cards and create your own stationary. There are lots of online printers that can offer you several hundred business cards for less than $30. Don't spend too much money on promotional material, just in case you decide not to go forward with your business.

7. Remember to File an Annual Report If Your State Requires One

Most states and countries require owners of LLCs to file annual reports (Arizona doesn't).

These are usually filed at the end of the year or on the anniversary of your formation date.

Most are easy to complete.

If you don't file one, the state or country could revoke your LLC charter, so be sure to remember this last and final step.

Obtaining Credit for Your LLC

As mentioned in Chapter 3, if you're a first-time rental property investor, your mortgage lender is unlikely to allow you to purchase the property under your LLC.

That's because your company doesn't have a financial track record.

It will take time to establish a good credit rating.

In the meantime, it's still a good idea to operate your business based on the future credit worthiness of your LLC. For a discussion on how to take title in the name of your LLC (an important asset protection strategy), see Garrett Sutton's *Loopholes of Real Estate.*[24]

When you lease your property, have the tenant sign a contract with your LLC, not with you personally. That can give you some protection from liability should something awful happen on your property. Although you'll have insurance to cover most liabilities, all policies have upper limits and doing business under a sole proprietorship could put your personal assets at risk.[25]

Also, when you do business with others (landscapers, repairmen, etc.), do it under your LLC name, not your personal name. Using your LLC for these transactions doesn't guarantee that someone won't come after your personal assets, but it could offer some protection. Always err on the side of caution.

Now, how are you going to get credit for your LLC?

Open a Business Credit Card

A good first step is to apply for a business credit card through your lending institution.

Use it for small purchases and pay off the balance every month, if you can.

---

24 Garrett Sutton, *Loopholes of Real Estate* (Scottsdale, AZ: RDA Press, 3rd edition, 2018).
25 I should emphasize that even with an LLC, you may be personally liable for adverse events on your property. For example, if the law requires your rental property to have a working smoke detector and you decide not to install one, your LLC and you personally can be held liable if a fire occurs and someone is injured. But if you install one correctly and it fails to function properly, your personal assets are generally protected.

Lenders and credit providers will review your LLC's credit reports and extend the offer of larger loans at better interest rates. But these perks are only available when you have a history of prompt repayment.

If your lending institution won't let you open a business credit card, try some of the online options. Capital One's Spark Classic business credit card, for example, is available to new businesses that have an average credit rating (it's widely considered the best card for new businesses).

If you still have difficulty opening a business credit card, try opening a "secured" business card. You give the lending institution $500 or more and you borrow from that. Paying it off every month helps you build credit. At the end of two years or sooner, the credit card companies will refund your deposit and give you an unsecured credit line. Note that some companies report your payment history to credit bureaus, but not all. Ask.

By the way, John tried unsuccessfully to obtain an unsecured business credit card, even though he had good credit and was able to obtain a $140,000 loan to purchase the rental property. He was denied credit in part because his business was new and had yet to file a tax return. He eventually obtained a secured business credit card.

Apply for a D-U-N-S Number

Another way to establish credit is to open a credit file through organizations such as Dun & Bradstreet.

D&B allows small business owners to apply for a D-U-N-S number, which tracks trade lines of credit and adds information to your report.

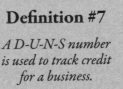

Definition #7

A D-U-N-S number is used to track credit for a business.

But to develop a credit history, you may have to pay them $800 or more. D&B then contacts your creditors and vendors to see if you're paying your bills on time. D&B then reports these results to any lending institutions or credit agencies you contact for loans or credit.

John applied for and obtained a D-U-N-S number. D&B called and tried to sell him its basic service. John decided to wait, for two reasons.

First, he figured he would need a couple of years of rental property experience to persuade a lending institution that his business was a good credit risk.

Second, John knew he would be paying higher interest rates on a business mortgage loan, which can cost 2 to 4 percent more than personal mortgage loans.

For the time being, he would use his personal credit to obtain loans to purchase rental properties. And then, when his investments were bigger and his financial risk higher, he would transition all aspects of the business under his LLC. But no matter how big your company becomes, most lenders still require a personal guarantee for the purchase of real estate.

Don't Let Them Pierce Your Corporate Veil

One final word of advice about your LLC.

To ensure your personal assets are protected, you must follow the laws and rules that govern LLCs in your state. The general rule is that your business must be a separate entity from you. That means that, at a minimum, you should:

1. *Keep good records;*
2. *Never mix personal and business monies (keep separate checking accounts);*
3. *Always file paperwork and pay fees required by state or federal law;*
4. *Conduct an annual meeting at least once a year, even if your state doesn't require it (the meeting doesn't have to long or formal, but create some minutes that address some of the issues or goals facing your company);*
5. *Always use or include the "LLC" when referring to your company (don't merge your business entity with your personal entity);*
6. *Never engage in fraudulent or illegal activities (I know you won't);*
7. *Hire an attorney when you need legal advice.*

If you fail to follow these rules, a court of law can issue an order that removes the "veil" of legal protection provided by your LLC, which means you will have to use your personal assets to satisfy a court judgment against your company and you.

For more details about creating and managing an LLC, see the Rich Dad Advisors books written by attorney Garrett Sutton: *Start Your Own Corporation* and *Loopholes of Real Estate* (both are 3rd editions and published by RDA Press of Scottsdale, Arizona.)

Chapter Five

Step 2: Get Your Investment Money

I bet some of you are probably itching to purchase a rental property. But you have a big problem.

Money.

Not enough of it, to be exact.

I won't lie to you.

It's not easy to purchase your first rental property without some cash or a down payment.

But it's not impossible.

Ten Ways to Finance Your Property Purchase

There are at least ten ways to secure investment money.

1. Use your home's equity.

Most people think of their home as an asset, not a liability.

John, my acquaintance who wanted to purchase a rental property, was among them.

His lifelong goal, like that of many Americans, was to pay off his house before retirement.

> **Tip #10**
>
> *An idle asset is better thought of as a liability.*

He succeeded.

And then he read some of my books, in which I point out that, when it comes to obtaining financial freedom, *an idle asset is better thought of as a liability—because the equity sits there, doing nothing.*

Sure, a home may appreciate in value every year.

But it doesn't keep pace with the returns on real estate rental property (see Chapter 2).

Most people are afraid to use the equity in their property to increase their financial worth, because they have been taught to believe "debt is bad."

Good vs. Bad Debt

There is bad debt, to be sure.

This includes high-interest payday or title loans and credit cards. If you have such debt, pay it off as soon as you can.

But debt is good when it's used to grow wealth.

> **Tip #11**
>
> *Debt is good when you leverage other people's money to invest in real estate and make money.*

I can even hear Gordon Gekko, the fictional character who declared in the movie *Wall Street* that "Greed... is good," declaring: "Debt is good, too!"

A failure to understand the difference between good and bad debt is what prevents many working-class and middle-class people from achieving financial independence.

Good debt is debt you obtain to leverage other people's money.

When you buy a rental property, you should put down as little as possible. If the sale price is $140,000, you normally will need to put down $35,000 to buy the property (25 percent of the total). The other $105,000 comes from the lending institution.

As the property appreciates in value (the average increase since 1940 is 6 percent per year), you make money off other people's money. At the end of the first year, you'll have (on paper) a property that is worth $8,400 more than when you purchased it. Most of that gain ($6,300 or 75 percent) comes from other people's money.

Types of Loans

John's story illustrates how an asset like a home can be leveraged.

He estimated he needed about $140,000 to purchase a small rental property. His home, which he owned outright, was worth about $250,000.

John had two options.

He could borrow $35,000 (using his home as collateral), use that as a down payment, and then ask a lending institution to loan him the $108,000 difference to purchase the rental property. But that meant he would pay closing costs on two different loans.

His better option was to borrow the entire $140,000, which collateralized the entire loan and meant he also would get a lower interest rate.

> **Definition #8**
>
> *A home equity line of credit (HELOC) has no closing costs and is a fast way to get cash, but the interest rate can be higher.*

This option also played well into John's long-term strategy: He would own the rental property outright and then use the equity in that property to leverage the purchase of another property.

He went to his bank and initially applied for a *home equity line of credit* (HELOC), which has no closing costs and is a fast way to get cash (usually under a week or two). But he learned that this type of loan often had to be repaid in twenty years or less and also had an *adjustable rate mortgage* (ARM) with a relatively high introductory interest rate (6.75 percent in his case—the average mortgage rate at the time was 4.2 percent).

> **Definition #9**
>
> *An adjustable rate mortgage (ARM) typically offers a lower interest rate, but the rate can be increased when market conditions change.*

The problem with an ARM is that the bank can adjust the interest rate on the loan (usually several years later) if the government increases the amount of money it lends to banks (usually under conditions of rising inflation).

Using an online *mortgage amortization calculator* (from amortization-calc.com/mortgage-calculator), John concluded it would be difficult for him to turn a positive cash flow on a property with an interest rate of 6.75 percent because the monthly payment would be much too high (about $820 a month). Also, if interest rates increased, his monthly mortgage payment would increase, placing more strain on cash flow.

> **Definition #10**
>
> *A traditional mortgage has closing costs but typically offers the lowest interest rate.*

John jettisoned that idea.

His bank then offered a twenty-year, 6.85 percent fixed-interest *home equity loan* that also had no closing costs. A fixed rate is often higher than an ARM, at least initially. But the interest rate was still too high in John's opinion. After all, he was putting his house up as collateral.

His bank then offered a thirty-year *cash-out refinance mortgage* at a rate of 4.5 percent.

Bingo!

The monthly payments were $550, about $270 less than the line of credit and equity loans.

Now he could generate a decent positive cash flow.

Another Advantage of Using Your Home's Equity to Finance a Rental Purchase

There's another big advantage in using the equity in your personal home to buy a rental property. You get to depreciate most closing costs, including origination fees, bank fees, title fees, and more.

Using the equity in your personal property to purchase a rental property can save you hundreds of dollars on your taxes and you can use the equity in your new property to purchase another property.

Okay, at this point, I know what many of you are thinking.

"John had lots of equity to buy a rental property. I have none. I have a modest-paying job. I just can't seem to get ahead. It's hard to save money."

Fortunately, home equity isn't the only way to raise money.

2. Borrow from your retirement funds.

Many private and government-funded retirement plans in America and around the world allow their owners to borrow from the equity in their retirement accounts.

In the United States, for example, investors with 401(k) plans may borrow $50,000 or 50 percent of the total amount of money in the fund (whichever is smaller).[26] That amount may not be enough to purchase an entire rental property, but it can be enough for a down payment.

There are some advantages to borrowing from your own funds. There is little or no cost to you. You are borrowing from yourself, so the interest you pay goes back to you. And your credit rating remains unaffected (ratings often go down after taking out a loan, because you are carrying more debt).

But there are some downsides, especially if you fail to repay the loan.

The first is that the loan payments can be hefty, because the loan usually has to be repaid in five years or less (or ten years in some cases when buying a home). A $35,000 loan at 6 percent interest for five years means your monthly payment will be $676.

If you're earning about 5 percent annually on your 401(k) investments, Bankrate.com's loan calculator[27] estimates that if you repay the loan in five years and you retire in five years, the cost of the loan to you is only $1,346. That's less than 1 percent interest per year. Excellent.

If you're twenty years from retirement, the cost is $2,800, which is less than 2 percent interest per year. Still not too bad.

But if you don't repay the loan, you're penalized 10 percent and your retirement fund will have $125,000 less in it in two decades.[28]

The upshot is that you need to repay that loan on time.

Be sure to talk to a 401(k) expert before borrowing from your fund.

---

26 Elizabeth O'Brien, "Here's What Happens When You Take out a Loan on Your 401(k)," *Marketwatch* (June 29, 2015), retrieved 10/2/19 from https://www.marketwatch.com/story/avoid-the-temptation-of-dipping-into-your-401k-2015-06-04/

27 The online calculator is available at https://www.bankrate.com/calculators/retirement/borrow-from-401k-calculator.aspx/

28 If you retire and still owe on the loan, you can continue to make payments or take the balance as a withdrawal. The latter is an attractive tax option if you are in a lower income bracket.

3. Live on your rental property.

This is called *house hacking* and is one of the easiest ways to purchase your first rental property.

You buy a duplex or a small multifamily (two to four units) property and move into one of the units and rent out the others. Ideally, the rent on your other units will cover your mortgage so you can live there rent-free.

When you move out, you have the option of selling or keeping the property.

Mortgage lenders generally require lower down payments on owner-occupied properties than on investment properties. There is less risk to the lenders, because they know property owners are less likely to default on their own home than on a rental unit.

You might even be able to qualify for an FHA (Federal Housing Administration) or VA (Veteran's Administration) loan, which requires little or no down payment.

> **Tip #12**
>
> *House hacking (living on your rental property) is one of the easiest ways to purchase your first rental property.*

Of course, talk to multiple lenders to get the best possible deal. Credit unions and savings and loan banks often have lower interest rates.

4. Find some partners.

If you have no money to invest but lots of time to manage a rental property, then consider looking for a partner who has a lot of money but no time.

I'm a big proponent of partnerships, even though I recognize they go sour sometimes.

Aside from bringing more capital into a business, I like working with partners because they are a good source of knowledge and advice. As the saying goes: *Two heads are better than one.*

To reduce the risk of a partnership going bad, you and your partner(s) need to clearly spell out in writing the roles each of you will play in the business. If one partner brings more cash to the deal or spends more time working on the property than the others, then that partner should be justly compensated. Otherwise, resentments build.

Once you establish the rules, you have to resist the temptation to judge whether you're being treated fairly. Good partnerships require trust.

In a best case scenario, each partner brings something unique to the relationship. My specialty has been property management. Other partners I've worked with are experts in construction, finance, real estate analysis, or law.

Irrespective of whether you actually get into a partnership, your long-term goal should focus on building a team of experts who can help you make good decisions. I'll talk more about that in the next chapter.

5. Find a lender who will finance 100 percent of the purchase price.

If you have a good credit rating and can find a rental property that is at least 20 percent undervalued, some lenders will finance the entire purchase.

The key here is finding the right property.

That can take time.

So have patience.

But as your business grows and demonstrates a successful track record, lenders and investors will loan money to you based not on the value of the property, but on the income-earning (business) potential of the property. Eventually, you won't have to put any money down.

6. Buy a rental property through a land contract.

Also called a *contract for deed*, this legal device means the seller becomes the lender, and he or she may not require any down payment.

You make monthly payments to the seller, not a bank or mortgage institution.

At the end of the payment period, you take full ownership of the home.

In the meantime, you get control over the property and normally will be responsible for maintenance and other costs, including paying the taxes (although legally the home will still be in the name of the seller).

> **Definition #11**
>
> *In a contract for deed, the seller becomes the lender.*

Under a land contract, you acquire an equitable interest in the property when you sign up. That equity grows as you continue to make monthly payments. In the meantime, as your equity increases, you may be able to secure a conventional loan and pay off the land contract, which gives you full ownership of the property.

The seller takes a risk because the selling price is set at the time the contract is executed. If the value of the property increases dramatically, the seller loses equity and you gain. If the value of the property drops, you, the buyer, could lose money.

As the buyer, you also must make the "rent/mortgage" payments every month. If you fail to do that, the seller can file a *land contract forfeiture*, which means all the money you paid to the seller for the property will be given to the seller—plus the seller keeps the real estate. You could lose everything.

In my opinion, land contracts work best between buyers and sellers who know and trust each other. For example, an older relative may wish to sell her property to a younger family member and use the monthly payments to supplement her income.

As a buyer, you should always do an inspection of the home and an appraisal before signing any agreement. I advise all parties to use attorneys when drafting a land contract to ensure everyone understands the terms of the agreement.

7. Find a rent-to-own property (lease with an option to buy).

A *rent-to-own agreement* contains two contracts: a standard lease agreement and an option to purchase.

The landlord retains title to the property until you, the tenant, exercise your option to purchase the property. At the beginning of the lease period, you normally negotiate a sale price for the property and you put down an *option fee*, which compensates the landlord should you back out of the deal.

> **Tip #13**
>
> *A rent-to-own contract can give you time to repair your credit and generate enough equity to cover the down payment.*

During the lease period, you typically pay higher rent than is the case for other similar properties. The extra rent money is applied toward the principal of the house or is placed into an *escrow account* (which means neither you nor the landlord can touch that money) until the time of purchase, when it's applied to reduce the purchase price. In either case, you build equity in the house.

> **Definition #12**
>
> *"Being in escrow" is a contract in which a third party, often a title company, receives and disburses money or property for the transacting parties.*

At the end of the lease period, which could be much longer than a year (e.g., five or even ten years), you have a right (option) to buy the property. And under the terms of the contract, much or all of the money you have paid in extra "rent" and the option fee is applied to the purchase of the property.

If you don't buy the property, you lose the option fee and the equity.

In a rent-to-own agreement, you, the renter, typically are responsible for making repairs. This is considered fair, because the tenant eventually will own the property.

You must also abide by any other rules set forth in the lease agreement.

If you violate those rules, the option can become null and void, which means you could lose everything toward the purchase of the property.

One advantage of a rent-to-own contract is that it can give you time to repair your credit and generate enough equity to cover the down payment on the property, which you can then use to qualify for a conventional mortgage to purchase the property at the end of the agreement.

As a renter-buyer, you should always do an inspection of the home and an appraisal before signing an agreement.

Of course, I also recommend you hire an attorney to check over the details of the contract.

8. Assume a seller's mortgage.

Some mortgage loans can be assumed by other people, which means you wouldn't have to provide a down payment. But the lender has to approve, and most mainstream mortgage companies don't allow this practice.

Nevertheless, it doesn't hurt to ask the seller if his or her mortgage can be assumed.

9. Negotiate a seller-held second mortgage.

If you have a lender who is willing to lend you most of the purchase price but you don't have enough money to cover the down payment, you might ask the seller to give you the money. You then make two separate mortgage payments.

Many lenders prohibit this practice, so find out before you put a lot of time into it.

10. Find some investors.

The difference between a partner and an investor is that a partner has ownership in the property. An investor's role usually is restricted to putting up money for the down payment on your rental property purchase. A mortgage company provides the rest.

> **Definition #13**
>
> *Passive income is income received on a regular basis, with little effort required to maintain it.*

The investor, like a mortgage lender, expects to be compensated for giving you the money. Usually the compensation is in the form of an interest rate that is higher than mortgage and open market rates.

The interest investors earn is called *passive income*, because the investors don't have to work to earn the money. IRS rules sometimes limit the amount of losses that an investor can claim on passive income (more on this Chapter 10).

Don't be afraid to ask your relatives, friends, and other people you know for money.

Many will turn you down.

But if you're a person of integrity and are known for paying people back when they loan you money, there's a good chance you can find some investors.

And if no one will loan you money, you haven't lost anything. (When you're wealthy, you can tell them, "I told you so.")

To enhance your chances of getting investors (even family members and friends), I recommend you develop a *business plan* that shows how much money you need, where you're going to get the rest of the money, how much the property costs, how much rent revenue and other sources of income it will generate, and how much it will cost to maintain the property.

Accredited vs. Unaccredited Investors

Before leaving the topic of investors, let me distinguish between two types: accredited and unaccredited.

An accredited investor is a person or organization that has substantial assets and/or income defined under U.S. law. For example, they must have: (1) a net worth of at least $1,000,000, excluding the value of one's primary residence; or (2) have income at least $200,000 each year for the last two years (or $300,000 combined income if married) and have the expectation to make the same amount this year; or (3) a trust with assets in excess of $5 million. Business and nonprofit organizations can also qualify as an "accredited investor" under Rule 501 of Regulation D of the U.S. Securities and Exchange Commission (SEC).

Unaccredited investors do not need to meet these criteria. Your non-wealthy family and friends would be classified as unaccredited investors.

There are advantages and disadvantages to each category. An accredited investor can often obtain a larger rate of return on her investment, but if the investment goes bust, she has less legal protection because she is expected under the law to be savvier about investing.

> **Definition #14**
>
> *An accredited investor is a person or organization with substantial assets or income.*

Most big-time real estate syndicators use only accredited investors, often because they have more funds to invest and the cost of processing those funds is less than it is with small-time investors. Your access to accredited investors generally will increase as your rental property portfolio builds.

Creating a Business Plan for Investors

You won't need a formal business plan if you plan to get your funding from family, friends, and business associates or colleagues. But you'll need a simple plan.

A business plan is like a promotional flier. Its goal is to convince others that you know what you're doing—that you have carefully thought out all of the details of a purchase.

> **Definition #15**
>
> *A business plan is a promotional flier and is needed to raise capital from accredited investors.*

It's not difficult to create a business plan for a small rental property purchase. Generally speaking, though, the bigger the project, the more information you'll need to provide. Your goal is to show that you can manage the investor's risk.

There is no one right way to create a business plan. In Text Box 5.1, I offer a general outline of the types of information you may want to include. If you're not sure whether to include something, add it in. Better to err on the side of caution.

> **Definition #16**
>
> *A proforma financial statement makes estimates of future expenditures and income.*

Most of the items in the plan are self-explanatory.

The last one, Section VIII, is called "Financial Proforma," or more formally the *proforma financial statement*. This simply involves making estimates of future expenditures and income, in contrast to financial statements that are based on actual past transactions.

The *proforma* statement is an ideal projection, meaning that it cannot account for unforeseen events, such as a depression or catastrophic disaster.

Text Box 5.1
Content for a Business Plan

A. *Front Cover:*
   1. A picture of the property under consideration
   2. The title of the report (example): The 12-Unit Apartment Complex on Main Street: A Multifamily Business Plan by (the name of your LLC).
B. *Section I - The Summary*
   1. A brief summary of the project, which includes the reasons why this is a good investment and how the purchase can benefit the community and investors.
   2. Financial overview
      a. Total costs of the purchase, including improvements needed (if any)
      b. Amount to be borrowed or already borrowed from mortgage lenders (include interest rates)
      c. Equity in the property (if any)
      d. Detailed list of improvements to be made (if any) and estimated value afterward
      e. How much investment money (down payment/cash for improvements) is needed
      f. Minimum investment required from each outside investor
      g. How much interest will be paid to investors and when their initial investment will be paid off
C. *Section II – The Property*
   1. Summary of Property: Number of units, types of floor plans, total square footage, additional pictures
   2. Amenities
      a. For the community as a whole (swimming pool, hot tub, clubhouse, etc.)
      b. For the units themselves (upgrades, storage, washer/dryer, etc.)
   3. Property Map (zoning, housing around the property, access to work, shopping and playgrounds, etc.)
   4. Floor Plans (if necessary)
D. *Section III – The Business Plan*
   1. Background of your company
   2. Who will manage the company (if you're not doing it directly yourself)
   3. When property will be refinanced (if applicable) and investors paid off (estimated dates)
   4. When the property will be sold (if applicable)
E. *Section IV – Legal Ownership*
   1. Who will own the property and how much will each partner/investor own?
   2. How profits/fees will be distributed to the owner(s) and investors
F. *Section V – Sales & Rent Comparisons*
   1. Sales information about similar properties, including year of construction, number of units, average size, total market valuation, price per unit and square foot, most recent sale date
   2. Rent information about other similar properties, including year built, number of units, average size, occupancy rate, asking rents, rent per square foot
G. *Section VII – Information about Your Business*
   1. LLC Overview and owners (provide a brief biography and picture)
   2. Number of properties owned and details
   3. Financial track record of the LLC
H. *Section VIII – The Financial Proforma*
   1. Projected costs (first five to eight years)
   2. Projected income (first five to eight years)

Chapter Six

Step 3: Find Your Ideal Market

Remember John, my acquaintance who obtained a cash-out refinance mortgage to purchase rental property worth up to $140,000?

He decided to look for a property in Sun City, Arizona, where only people aged fifty-five and over can live.

At first glance, this decision might seem a bit foolish, because the rental market seems so restricted. But John had several good reasons to buy there.

1. *Older renters tend to be more credit worthy than younger population groups.* In other words, they pay their rents on time.

2. *The neighborhoods are clean and beautiful.* Deed covenants and homeowners association rules require residents to keep their yards clean and tidy. John wouldn't have to worry about the neighbors dumping old cars and junk in their yards, which could adversely affect the value of his property.

3. *Property values in Sun City have risen about 9 percent per year during the past five years.* By comparison, Scottsdale, a community with many higher-priced homes, was rising at an average of 4 percent per year.

4. *Property taxes are much less in Sun City,* because the residents don't have to pay school taxes.

5. *Sun City is one of the safest communities in America.* The crime rate is extremely low. Older people want to live in a safe place.

6. *National market reports show rental demand among the fifty-five-plus market is growing much faster than it is for other groups.* That's partly because baby boomers are retiring in record numbers.

7. *Demand for rental properties in Sun City is high,* because covenants and HOA agreements limit the number of rental properties in many areas of the community.

Of course, there were some drawbacks to buying in Sun City.

A new buyer has to pay a $3,500 one-time "Preservation & Improvement" fee (*ouch!*) and a $300 ownership transfer fee. Owners also must pay an Annual Property Assessment of $496, which enables them or their renters to use the many recreational facilities in the community (eight golf courses, six swimming pools, four fitness facilities, thirty bowling lanes, and lots of arts and crafts clubs, etc.). Fortunately, these costs are either depreciable or tax deductible for landlords.

Another disadvantage to renting in Sun City is that many tenants are on fixed incomes, so they are very sensitive to increases in rent. Many landlords keep the rents "artificially" low until the tenant moves out.

There is no such thing as the perfect property.

There are always trade-offs.

An area of high rental demand almost always has more expensive properties. A less expensive neighborhood usually means the rents are lower and the renters will have less-than-stellar credit histories.

The key is to find a property that meets your specific needs, which may change over time as you build your rental portfolio.

In this chapter, I'll help you find the right market for your rental property purchase. In the next chapter, I'll show you how to find the right property within that market.

Real Estate Research Is Fun

Before you hire a real estate agent and start looking for properties, you might want to take some time to do some preliminary research from the comfort of your home computer.

Research can be fun.

Did I really say that?

Yes, and I meant it.

Just think of yourself as a detective.

Your "case" is to find the right property for the right price in the right market—and to do it swiftly to beat your competition. There are far more real estate investors out there than good deals. That's why you need to research. Knowledge gives you an edge.

The first and most important principle in searching for a rental property is this, and please don't forget it: *The market is more important than the property.*

Properties in areas where property values are decreasing or increasing at a much slower rate than other areas often are not a good

> **Tip #14**
>
> *The market is more important than the property.*

investment. Unfortunately, too many real estate investors buy real estate based on a gut feeling—"I just know this area is going to appreciate in value."

This intuitive approach is too risky.

You need to evaluate markets in general (usually a city or metropolitan area) and submarkets (the neighborhood or areas in which you want to purchase). Ideally, *look for markets where the supply of rental housing is low and demand is high.* Supply is the number of rental properties that are available. Demand is the number of people looking to rent.

Supply is fairly easy to figure out. Tax and building records offer such information.

Demand is harder to assess. My teams and I do it by examining occupancy rates in cities and

> **Tip #15**
>
> *Look for markets where the supply of rental housing is low and demand is high.*

neighborhoods. The higher the rates, the higher the demand.

The U.S. Census publishes statistics on occupancy rates by city (see census.gov/newsroom/press-releases/2019/hvs.html). The statistics aren't refined enough to search by zip code area, but they do have statistics on state, city, and metropolitan areas, and the general numbers can be useful to even small investors.

For example, the statistics show that vacancy rates in the Phoenix area remained relatively unchanged from 2015 to 2018 (about 6 percent per year), but the vacancy rates declined in Tucson, going from 10 to 4 percent.

Why?

Because other statistics show that the city's population grew and the number of permits to build new housing and apartment units dropped from 2008 to 2016 (see https://www.huduser.gov/portal/publications/pdf/TucsonAZ-comp-16.pdf).

Another indicator of demand is the number of specials being offered to lure people to rent. If many apartment communities in an area are offering specials, that usually means supply is high and demand is low. Be cautious.

Three Drivers of Supply and Demand

As I've pointed out in my other writings, three factors drive supply and demand for rental properties: *employment, resources,* and *location*.

Employment

People flock to areas where jobs are plentiful.

In general, apartment dwellers want to be closer to where they work than homeowners. The latter will drive farther because affordable housing is often in the outlying areas of big cities. These "bedroom communities" frequently are not good places to invest in rental properties.

> **Fact #8**
>
> *Three key drivers of rental market supply and demand are employment, resources, and location.*

High employment areas generally attract rental property investments, but don't ignore the big picture. Communities with lots of jobs can have an oversupply of rental housing. Stability in a community is also important. Houston grew quickly during the oil industry boom in the 1980s and then market conditions tanked, putting lots of people out of work who, in turn, left many rental units vacant.

Resources

Resources also attract people.

Venice Beach in California has a beach and a hip population; Aspen in Colorado has skiing and great views; and Scottsdale in Arizona has golf, sun, and shopping.

Military bases, sports arenas, universities, large businesses, casinos, and new highways or extensions also can be considered resources. As they grow, so does the demand for rental housing.

Be cautious, though. If the area is too dependent upon one resource and that resource closes down or goes sour, so does everything else. Military base closures have wiped out many businesses and real estate investors.

The upshot of all this is that social and economic diversity is generally a good thing. The market tends to be more stable.

> **Tip #16**
>
> *Diversity in businesses and resources generally creates more stability in a market.*

High-priced housing also can help real estate investors. If housing in an area is too expensive, renting becomes more attractive (and generally produces higher rental rates and cash flow).

Location

The final driver of demand for rental property is *location*—the specific area surrounding the property itself. If your desired property is near a busy road, then you have what I call "drive-by visibility" for the "For Rent" sign you pitch on the property. This is an inexpensive way to advertise vacancies.

In terms of location, also be sure to look at crime rates and poverty levels. Although some real estate investors have gotten rich renting properties in depressed areas, they take on a lot of management problems and headaches. Property values in high crime/high poverty areas also don't increase as quickly, and you likely will have more difficulty selling your property.

Three Levels of Research

In my previous writings, I introduced three levels of research.

Level One involves looking at a market as a whole, trying to find demographic and market trends that favor investment; *Level Two* involves meeting and talking with real estate professionals, including sales agents, landlords, and anyone else who can provide more precise information about the market; and *Level Three* involves selecting who will be on your team long-term in that particular market and provide you with market information.

For your first purchase, you definitely will engage in Level One and Level Two research. Level Three will come in to play when you purchase more properties and need more help to find and manage them.

Level One

Even without conducting any research, John knew that the Phoenix area was a good place to invest.

Although the Phoenix market has had its share of ups and downs, people keep moving there because it offers many resources and amenities.[29] The list includes sunshine (87 percent of the year), great places to see and travel (Grand Canyon, mountains, Sedona), and leisure-time activities (Phoenix alone has nearly 200 golf courses and dozens of top-notch resorts). Many people come to Phoenix to get out of the cold, snowy winters back home.

But John didn't know much about Sun City itself.

Was it a good place to purchase a rental property?

So he began, like I often do, by researching on the internet.

He typed "Property values in Sun City Arizona" into a search engine.

The first listing (ignoring all of the "ads" listed before it) was Zillow, a website that lures home buyers and sellers. Zillow listed Sun City as a "very hot" market, or a seller's market—

> **Tip #17**
>
> *Zillow, Trulia, Realtor.com and other online real estate websites are good places to start researching a market.*

---

29 Phoenix was the fastest growing metropolitan area in 2018.

there are more buyers than sellers, and so prices tend to be higher.[30] The median home sale price in Sun City was $168,000 in January 2019, which is 24 percent less than home values in the entire Phoenix metropolitan area. Home values in Sun City have increased an average of 10.3 percent since 2012. Over that eight-year time period, prices increased 119 percent, from $76,600 to $168,000.

The median sales price tracks closely with the assessed valuations of the homes, which are set by the Maricopa County Assessor.[31] The assessed valuations are lower, however, as they usually are in most places in America. Some analysts argue that the assessed valuations are lower because assessors are wary of over valuing properties, which produces a lot of complaints from property owners.[32]

The median rent price in Sun City was $1,288 (about ninety cents per square foot), which is lower than the $1,595 average for the rest of the Phoenix metropolitan area. Only 4.8 percent of Sun City homes sold with a negative equity, compared with 8.2 percent nationally. The delinquency rate on mortgages is 0.3 percent, much less than the national average of 1.1 percent.

Wow, all of that information from just two clicks, and it only took a couple of minutes.

John was encouraged.

He found another website called "Neighborhood Scout," which included information about demographics, real estate, crime, and schools. John learned that property values in the middle of Sun City and north of Bell Road were appreciating the fastest. Properties on the south side of the city, particularly below Grand Avenue, were appreciating, too, but at a slightly slower rate. Crime was low in the city but even lower in the higher appreciation areas.

---

30 Data retrieved 10/3/2019 from https://www.zillow.com/sun-city-az/home-values/.

31 The assessed valuation data presented in the chart is lagged one year, because the assessor sets the values for 2019 in 2018. The data are available at https://www.mcassessor.maricopa.gov/data-sales/ reports.php; click on "Reports and Data."

32 Mark Engebretson and David Demers, "Assessing Damage: Unfair Property Tax Assessments Cause Working-class Homeowners and Renters to Pay Too Much, While Owners of Businesses, Farms, and Expensive Homes Don't Pay Enough," Twin Cities Reader (March 20-26, 1991), pp. 10-13.

John also learned that not all of the information on the website was accurate. The map incorrectly constructed the boundaries around Sun City. Errors abound on the internet. That's why it's wise to look to multiple sources for information.

Trulia, another online site, showed that property values in Sun City had increased more than 50 percent in the last five years. The median rent, as Zillow also reported, was $1,200 for a two-bedroom home or condominium. This statistic was based on the number of landlords that put free ads on the Trulia site (the company makes much of its money from real estate agents who advertise there).

> **Tip #18**
>
> *Many counties with metropolitan areas offer online sites where citizens and investors can obtain tax and assessment histories of properties.*

Trulia also showed that rent rates increased $100 a month from June to August—a 9 percent increase. Landlords apparently increased rates just before the busy fall and winter season started up. So the going rent rate would be $1,300 when John made his purchase.

Many other websites provide information about Sun City, but you get the picture. You can learn a lot about a market in just an hour of research on the internet.

Level Two

John's real estate agent was not intimately familiar with Sun City, but she talked with other agents and learned that not all properties, including single family homes, are available to rent out.

Deed covenants and Homeowners Associations (HOAs) often prevent owners from renting their property. This prohibition applied particularly to higher priced areas and to condominium, duplex, and town home communities. But single family homes in older areas were not under such restrictions.

At first glance, this looks like a negative. But, remember, you want to find markets where demand is high and supply is low. That combination pushes monthly rental rates up and keeps your property at full occupancy.

John also learned through his real estate agent that many of the properties in older sections of Sun City have sewer lines that are disintegrating. Fixing them can cost $3,000 or more. So he decided to pay for an inspection of the sewer system before making his purchase.

Level Three

If you are a real estate agent, you obviously won't need a broker or agent.

> **Tip #19**
>
> *If you are buying a home for rent, be sure the deed covenants and homeowners associations allow rentals.*

But John wasn't one, so he initially consulted a close friend who had a license.

Nothing wrong with that.

A friend is a person you can trust.

I'm sure you know that not all real estate agents always work in the best interests of their clients. So, if you don't have an agent, I encourage you to ask friends, business associates, and relatives for referrals. The same goes for other people you hire. Referrals are far more credible than online ratings.

To buy your first property, you also will need to hire a property inspection expert and maybe an appraiser. The inspector's goal is to find as many things wrong with the property as possible. You then know exactly what you're buying. That inspection can also put pressure on the seller to make repairs or lower the sale price.

Real estate agents often recommend property inspectors. Be cautious, though, because agents don't get paid unless the sale closes, and an inspector who gets a lot of business from an agent may soft-peddle some problems to keep their clients happy. You want an inspector who works for you and only you.

An appraiser is optional unless you're taking out a mortgage, in which case your lender will handle the details. The lender wants to ensure that its investment money is going into a valuable asset. If you're paying cash for the property and are uncertain about its market value, then hire an appraiser. It will cost about $500 but it could save you thousands of dollars.

In fact, studies of appraisers after the 2008 housing downturn showed that they tended to inflate the values of properties to ensure the real estate deal would close. Since then, the industry put some rules into place to reduce this problem, but as a buyer, it's still best if you find an appraiser who is independent of the people in a property deal.

You don't normally need to hire an attorney or an accountant to purchase a rental house or condominium, especially if the property has not yet been used as a rental unit. But if you're purchasing an apartment community, you may need to consult these professionals when looking at legal issues or for help examining the seller's bookkeeping records. You need to be sure the property is making money, as the seller contends.

> **Tip #20**
>
> *You may not need an accountant or attorney on your first rental property purchase, but as your business grows you will need a team to help you make good decisions.*

If you purchase a rental home or small multifamily unit, you don't need to hire an accountant. You just need to keep track of expenses and income. Keep copies of all receipts. If the IRS audits you, it will disallow any expense that isn't documented.

At the end of the year, you can do your own taxes. It's not difficult, thanks to home and business tax software, which is inexpensive and easy to use. It will save you hundreds of dollars in accountant fees. (I'll talk about this later in Chapter 10.)

When you reach the big time and are buying large apartment communities, you'll need to add more team members to help you navigate legal and financial matters. In many cases, the advice you get will save you more money than the cost of the advice.

Chapter Seven

Step 4: Find Your Ideal Property

John's initial search suggested to him that Sun City was good place to buy.

But could he purchase a two-bedroom rental property and turn a profit with a monthly lease fee of $1,300, which is the average rental rate for single-family properties in the community?

There is a *tipping point* at which the price of a rental property will outstrip its rental income. If the mortgage and maintenance on a property cost $2,000 a month and the average rent charged for similar properties was $1,000, John would incur a hefty negative cash flow.

He needed to identify that tipping point: How much house could he buy and still afford to pay all of the estimated expenses (mortgage payment, taxes, fees, maintenance, and utilities) and turn a positive cash flow?

Estimate Your Cash Flow

The first step in estimating cash flow on a property is to calculate the mortgage payment.

As a rule of thumb, *I recommend the mortgage payment on homes be no more than two-thirds of the total rent payment. That's because the rest of the income is needed to cover the*

> **Tip #21**
>
> *Mortgage payments on small rental properties should be no more than two-thirds of the total rent payment.*

costs of taxes, insurance, fees, and maintenance, as well as provide at least some positive cash flow.

Because the average two-bedroom Sun City home rented for $1,300, that meant John's mortgage payment (interest and principal only) should not exceed $870 a month.

To estimate his payment, he used an online mortgage calculator. Scores of them are out there. Most sites bombard you with ads. Some will even ask for your email address and phone number to use the calculator. Avoid those unless you want to get a lot of emails.

John found a simple calculator at *amortization-calc.com/mortgage-calculator*. He didn't have to give his email address. To calculate a mortgage payment, the site requested four pieces of information:

1. *Loan Type*
   A click of this button gives three options: Mortgage, Refinance or Equity. It doesn't matter which of these you select. The results are the same. The categories are used for advertising. Selecting "mortgage" produces the largest number of lenders, followed by "refinance." No one advertises on the "equity" page, probably because equity loans usually come from the lender that already has your main mortgage—after all, you can't shop for a different lender.

2. *Home Price*
   Type in the estimated maximum amount of the money you think you can obtain to purchase a rental property. If your mortgage institution requires 25 percent down and you have $50,000 on hand, then type in $150,000, which is the maximum you can borrow. That means you can buy a $200,000 property. Increase or reduce the loan sum as needed.

3. *Loan Term*
   How many years, months, or weeks do you need to pay back the loan? The standard is thirty years, and most investors prefer that because the monthly loan payments are lower. Some investors prefer fewer years because they will pay less interest (of course,

their overall monthly payment will be higher), but they are not taking full advantage of leverage.

4. *Interest Rate*

Enter the amount offered at your lending institution or just estimate. You can find the national average mortgage interest rate by going to a government website managed by the Federal Reserve (https://fred. stlouisfed.org/series/MORTGAGE30US). Your actual rate will be lower or higher based on several factors, including your credit rating, how much you put down, and how many *mortgage points* you buy. Points (also known as loan origination fees) are paid directly to the lender at closing to obtain a reduced interest rate. The process is often referred to as "buying down the rate"—you basically are paying interest on the loan in advance. One point costs 1 percent of your loan amount, or $1,000 for every $100,000. In general, avoid paying points, as they decrease your leverage. Points must be depreciated over the length of the loan (usually thirty years), because the law will not let you prepay interest in a single year.[33]

John spent about an hour calculating different rates, adjusting both the amount needed and the interest rate. He eventually concluded that a $140,000, thirty-year fixed-interest cash-out refinance mortgage loan at 4.5 percent interest was a good fit. It generated a monthly mortgage payment of $709, which was 59 percent of the total purchase price and lower than the two-thirds rule. During the first year of payments, about $521 would go to interest and $188 to principal.[34]

As time passes, the interest amount decreases slowly and the principal increases. During the first year, the mortgage payments would generate about $2,259 in equity ($188 x 12), assuming a tenant occupies the property.

---

33 The law is more complicated when the amount of points paid exceeds $7,500. See IRS Form 4562, *Depreciation and Amortization*. There are also limitations on interest deductions by landlords earning $25 million or more. (Wouldn't that be a nice problem to have?)

34 Note that John is not leveraging this purchase, because he took out a cash-out refinance mortgage on his home. But he will leverage his next purchase. He will use the equity in his rental home to put a down payment on his next purchase. I'll discuss this in later chapters.

Now it was time to estimate all of John's expected expenses. He created eight categories:

1. *Mortgage*
   As discussed above, John estimated his payments would be $709 a month. He wouldn't have to pay mortgage insurance because his loan would be fully collateralized by his home.

2. *Taxes*
   What are the taxes on a $140,000 home in Sun City? John went to Zillow.com (there are several other real estate online services that provide similar information) and did a search of two-bedroom homes in Sun City that recently sold for exactly $140,000. About thirty homes popped up. He then randomly selected seven and clicked on the links to find the most recent tax bills on those homes: $631, $548, $513, $503, $487, $457 and $327. Adding those amounts and dividing by seven gave him an average yearly rate of $495. (Add more properties to the numerator if you want a more precise figure.) So taxes would cost about $41 a month ($495 ÷ 12).

3. *Insurance*
   John's insurance company gave him an estimate of $500 a year for a single-family detached rental property in Sun City and $270 for a condominium. Both offered $100,000/$300,000 coverage, which means $100,000 per person for bodily injuries sustained in one incident and topping out at a maximum payout of $300,000 for all claims. The policies also cover the costs of repairing or rebuilding the homes if they are damaged or destroyed. Condominium owners pay less for insurance than single family detached homes because the outside walls and roof are usually insured by the Homeowners Association, which covers the cost with HOA fees charged to condominium owners. The upshot is that they pay about the same amount as homeowners.

4. *Advertising*
   Landlords can advertise their rental units on Zillow, Trulia, and other online websites for free. These sites have become effective

places for finding tenants, according to landlords John talked with. But as a back-up plan, John intended to purchase a rent sign to put up on the lawn. He allocated $25 to buy the sign ($2 a month).

5. *Recreation Fee*

   The community of Sun City charges a $496 yearly recreation fee on all properties, which comes to about $41 a month ($496 ÷ 12). This fee helps maintain the seven recreational facilities in the entire community, which includes golf courses, swimming pools, and arts, crafts, and hobby centers.

6. *Gas/Electric Utilities*

   John's tenant would be responsible for gas and electricity, but when the home is vacant John would have to pay the utilities. He estimated the property would be vacant one month out of the year. Because Sun City homes tend to be small (under 1,400 square fee), John estimated the combined gas/electric bills would average only $100 a month. That comes to about $8 a month.

7. *Water/Sewer/Trash*

   Most landlords pay the water, sewer, and trash services. Part of the reason is to ensure that if a tenant fails to pay these bills, the services won't be turned off. You can imagine what would happen if the toilets could not be flushed or the trash were not picked up. Water, sewer, and trash bills in Sun City average $68 a month.

8. *Routine Maintenance/Repairs*

   Maintenance costs are difficult to predict. But real estate experts say you should put aside about 1 percent of the total value of the property each year,[35] which is $1,400 in this case, or about $120 a month.

9. *Reserve/Contingency Fund*

   For big expenses, such as replacing an air conditioning unit, it's best to set aside some money each month. John allocated $90 a month, about 7 percent of the total monthly rental rate.

---

35 Source: Zillow: https://www.zillow.com/blog/investing-101-estimating-rental-property-expenses-94824/

Table 7.1 sums up John's expected expenses on a $140,000 rental property.

Table 7.1
Monthly Estimated Costs of a $140,000 Rental Property

Expense	Home
1. Mortgage	$709
2. Taxes	$41
3. Insurance	$42
4. Advertising	$2
5. Annual recreation fee	$41
6. Gas/Electric (when unit is unoccupied)	$8
7. Water/sewer/trash	$68
8. Routine maintenance/repair/landscaping	$120
9. Reserve/Contingency fund	$90
Totals	$1,121
Estimated Monthly Rental Rate	$1,300
Estimated Monthly Cash Flow	**$179**

He expected to incur about $1,121 in monthly costs ($13,452 annually) for a two-bedroom $140,000 home in Sun City.

If tenants occupy his property for the entire year, he will generate $15,600 in rental income ($1,300 x 12), which means his cash flow will be about $179 a month (or $2,148 a year). That's not a lot of profit—but remember, over the next year John will earn equity through principal payments ($2,259) and appreciation ($10,640).

Estimate Your Five-Year and Ten-Year Gains

No one can predict the future of markets and housing.

But economists point out that the best predictor of future activity is past activity.

Like most real estate investors, John wanted an estimate of what his investment would look like in five and ten years.

So he needed to find housing and renting statistics in Sun City.

There are lots of sources for this information, but he used Zillow, because it's easy to access and doesn't cost anything.

As I pointed out in the second chapter, equity for a rental property is built through three major things: (1) appreciation, (2) cash flow, and (3) principal payments. The third one depends on the interest rate of your loan and payment schedule. He already has that info (about $188 a month in principal payments on the loan in the first year).

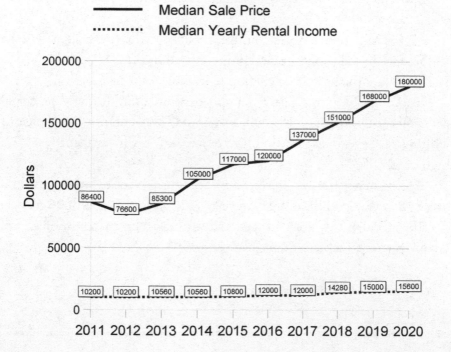

Figure 7.1 - Median Sale Price and Rent in Sun City
From 2011 to 2020

—— Median Sale Price
·········· Median Yearly Rental Income

Figure 7.1 shows the data he retrieved from Zillow.[36]

From January 2011 to January 2020, the median sale price of a property in Sun City went from $86,400 to $180,000. That's a 108 percent increase over the ten-year period, or an average of 7.6 percent per year.

During the same time period, average monthly rental rates also grew, but at a slower pace. The graph shows that the typical renter in Sun City paid $10,200 a year in rent in 2011 ($850 a month), compared with $15,600 in 2020 ($1,300 a month). That's a 52 percent increase, or an average of 4.3 percent per year.

Now all John had to do was to put this data into a table similar to the one I presented in Chapter 2 (see Table 2.1).

Table 7.2 shows the results.

After paying all taxes and expenses, John can expect to earn $205,265 in profits on this property in ten years. This figure assumes that future trends in Sun City are roughly the same as the previous ten years.

Of course, there are no guarantees.

He could earn more or less.

But this is the single best estimate he can make, and he was very pleased.

At the end of ten years, the total value of his investment will be $345,265. The value of his rental property will increase from $140,000 to $291,240 (see the bottom of column C in table).

In the first year, his gain from appreciation, cash flow and principal payments (columns C+D+E) will be $15,047 (see column B). The gains will increase every year until, in the tenth year, his investment reaches a high of $27,093.

If John owned five properties, his total gains (profits) before taxes would exceed $1 million at the end of ten years ($205,265 x 10 = $1,026,325).

The moral of this story is that you don't need a big cash flow or a lot of big properties to achieve financial freedom.

---

36 Data compiled by Zillow.com, retrieved from https://www.zillow.com/sun-city-az/home-values/

Table 7.2
Expected Gains from John's $140,000 Investment in 10 Years
(Based on Past Appreciation and Rent Price Trends in Sun City, Arizona)

Column =	A	B	C	D	E
Year	Cumulative Gains by Year (B1+B2+...)	Gains by Year (C+D+E)	Equity from Appreciation (7.6% Per Year)*	Cash Flow (4.3% rent increase per year)*	Equity from mortgage payments**
1	$15,047	$15,047	$10,640	$2,148	$2,259
2	$31,098	$16,051	$11,449	$2,240	$2,362
3	$48,224	$17,126	$12,318	$2,337	$2,471
4	$66,500	$18,276	$13,255	$2,437	$2,584
5	$86,008	$19,508	$14,263	$2,542	$2,703
6	$106,832	$20,824	$15,346	$2,651	$2,827
7	$129,067	$22,235	$16,513	$2,765	$2,957
8	$152,811	$23,744	$17,767	$2,884	$3,093
9	$178,172	$25,361	$19,118	$3,008	$3,235
10	$205,265	$27,093	$20,571	$3,138	$3,384
Total Gains =	$205,265	$205,265	$151,240	$26,150	$27,875
Total Value =	$345,265	Total Value of Property =	$291,240		

*The 7.6% appreciation estimate and 4.3% rent increases rates are derived from data compiled by Zillow for the previous 10 years and are compounded.

**Based on a 30-year fixed rate mortgage loan at 4.5% interest. The original loan amount is $140,000 and amortization tables were used to calculate the interest and principal payments. After 10 years, the principal balance on the loan is $112,125.

But if you're looking for even better returns, you might consider buying a small apartment community because they offer economies of scale. In other words, the cost of purchasing a four-unit apartment community is much less than four individual homes,[37] and it generates nearly the same amount of revenue.

Buying small multi-unit rental properties is the subject of my next book in this series.

Three Recommendations Before You Buy

John is ready to buy a property.

But I have three recommendations for him before he signs the closing papers.

1. Always hire a professional to inspect the home for problems

You've heard the old saying, "Beauty is skin deep."

That idiom applies to buying rental property as well.

A home may look wonderful on the inside and out, but serious problems may be lurking.

In Sun City, many unsuspecting buyers have been shocked to learn that the sewer pipes running from older homes to the street are deteriorating. The cost of replacing them can easily exceed $3,000.

When John was searching for a property in Sun City, he found a house that needed a lot of fix up but was selling for a great price.

The seller disclosed that one of the areas around a vent on the roof had been leaking. No big deal until John inspected the roof. A ten-by-ten area on the gray asphalt roof was black. Was that mold? If so, the cost of removing the mold and replacing the roof underneath could run into the thousands of dollars.

High quality home inspectors can charge $500 or more, but they can save you thousands of dollars and that helps you sleep at night.

---

37 A four-unit apartment community costs less to build than four homes because the units share walls and roofs. In addition, closing costs are less, because you close on just one property rather than four. And maintenance costs are less, because the apartment community likely occupies less total ground space and you don't have to drive to four different properties.

You need to do *due diligence* before signing a purchase contract (more on this later).

2. Be cautious before hiring a property management company

Many owners of rental homes hire property management companies to manage their properties, which can include finding tenants. But these companies can charge as much as 30 percent of the total rental fee.

A fee that high would put John in the hole. Fortunately, he didn't have to hire someone, because he's also a handyman and wanted to personally manage the property.

In general, you need to purchase a property that generates a higher cash flow to justify the hiring of a property management company. Usually this means an apartment community that contains at least four and maybe a half dozen units.

> **Tip #22**
>
> *Hiring a property management company works best when you have a strong cash flow.*

Also, you need to do your homework when selecting a company. Some are not diligent. Get references from real estate agents, lawyers, accountants, and even tenants. The more referrals, the better.

3. Don't buy unless you find the property that meets your needs

John waited two months for his refinance mortgage to be approved. (The bank made some mistakes.)

During that time, he watched as more than two dozen properties in Sun City came on the market and were quickly sold. Prices of newer properties coming onto the market were higher, and there were fewer of them.

When he finally had the money, there were only a few properties in his price range, and none looked attractive.

But he was patient.

Several months later, he found one.

John was fortunate, but what happens if you're looking for a property and can't find one that meets your needs?

Be proactive.

If you see a property you like, go online to the county assessor's or treasurer's office and look it up. You'll find the names of the owners, the deed, taxes, tax history, sales history, and lots more. All of this information is public data. You also can get a ballpark price for the home through Zillow or Trulia.

You could send a letter to the owner and say you're interested in buying the property. Be sure to tell them you're not one of those real estate companies that offers low-ball prices or high fees. You are willing to pay full market value. But don't make an offer until you inspect the property.

Make Your Offer

Lots of books and articles give investors advice about how to negotiate a real estate contract. Some promote the idea that getting a good deal depends a lot on knowing the motivations of the seller and your ability to negotiate.

Maybe.

But my philosophy transcends that puffery and focuses on the most important question: *At what price is the property going to turn a profit for you?*

When you're ready to make an offer on a property, don't get too wrapped up into trying to figure out the motivations of the seller or how you can outwit her or him. Base your offer on a price that will turn a profit for you.

> **Definition #17**
>
> *A purchase agreement is a sales contract – an offer to purchase a property.*

Then your real estate agent will draft a sales contract, better known as a *purchase agreement*, to present to the seller and/or their agent (see sample on next page). Although it looks complicated, it's not. The first part identifies the location of the property and the legal description. There are ten more elements or so, depending upon the property and the needs of the buyer and seller.

Text Box 7.1 – First Page of Typical Purchase Agreement

SAMPLE AGREEMENT TO PURCHASE REAL ESTATE

The undersigned (herein "Purchaser") hereby offers to purchase from the owner (herein "Seller") the real estate located at _____ in the city of_____, County of_____, State of_____, the legal description of which is:_____ ____ upon the following terms and conditions:

1. Purchase Price and Conditions of Payment
The purchase price shall be_____Dollars ($_____) to be paid in accordance with subparagraph _____, below:
A: Cash. The purchase price shall be paid in its entirety in cash at the time of closing the sale. B: Cash Subject to New Mortgage. The purchase price shall be paid in cash at the time of closing the sale subject, however, to Purchaser's ability to obtain a first mortgage loan within _____days after the acceptance of this offer by Seller in the amount of $_____, payable in not less than _____monthly installments, including interest at a rate not to exceed_____% financing. If such financing cannot be obtained within the time specified above then either Purchaser or Seller may terminate this agreement and any earnest money deposited by Purchaser will be promptly refunded. C: Cash Subject to Existing Mortgage. The purchase price shall be paid in cash at the time of closing the sale after deducting from the purchase price the then outstanding balance due and owing under the existing mortgage in favor of _____, dated _____, 20___, in the original amount of $_____; of such mortgage debt is approximately $_____ as of _____, 20____. D: Cash With Assumption of Existing Mortgage. The purchase price shall be paid in cash at the time of the closing of the sale after deducting from the purchase price the then outstanding balance due and owing under the existing mortgage in favor of _____, dated _____, 20___,having a present balance of approximately $_____, as of _____, 20___, which the purchaser hereby assumes and agrees to pay in accordance with its terms and to perform all of its provisions; purchaser shall pay any and all payments coming due after the closing of the sale. Any transfer fees required by the mortgage shall be paid by_____. E: Sale by Land Contract. The purchase price shall be paid in accordance with the certain land contract attached hereto and incorporated into this contract by this reference. The down payment to be made at the time of closing this sale shall be $_____and the balance of $_____shall be paid at the rate of _____% per annum.

2. Earnest Money Deposit
As earnest money Purchaser deposits $_____with the broker which shall be applied to the purchase price at the time of closing the sale. In the event that this offer is not accepted by Seller this earnest money deposit shall be promptly refunded to Purchaser by the broker. In the event that this offer is accepted by Seller and Purchaser shall fail to perform the terms of this agreement the earnest money deposit shall be forfeited as and for liquidated damages suffered by Seller. Seller is not, however, precluded from asserting any other legal or equitable remedy, which may be available to enforce this agreement.

3. Real Estate Taxes, Assessments, and Adjustments
Real Estate Taxes accrued against the property shall be prorated through the date of closing the sale and Seller shall pay all taxes allocated to the property through that date of acceptance of this offer to purchase. Rents, if any, shall be prorated through the date of closing and all rent deposits shall be transferred to Purchaser. Existing casualty insurance shall be canceled/prorated through the date of closing.

4. Title to the Property
Seller shall provide purchaser prior to the closing and promptly after the acceptance of this offer, at Seller's expense and at Seller's option an abstract of title to the property brought down to date or an owner's policy of title insurance in an amount equal to the purchase price, said abstract of policy to show marketable or insurable title to the real estate in the name of Seller subject only to easements, zoning and restrictions of record and free and clear of all other liens and encumbrances except as stated in this offer. If the abstract or title policy fails to show marketable or insurable title in Seller a reasonable time shall be permitted to cure or correct defects. Seller shall convey title to Purchaser at the time of closing by a good and sufficient general warranty deed free and clear of all liens and encumbrances except as otherwise provided in this offer and subject to easements, zoning and restrictions of record.

5. Possession of the Property
Purchaser shall be given possession of the property on _____, 20____. A failure on the part of Seller to transfer possession as specified will not make Seller a tenant of Purchaser, but in such event Seller shall pay to

1. **Purchase price and conditions of payment.** The amount you're offering for the property and the conditions of payment are the first two items of the contract. Most sellers prefer cash, because the deal closes quickly and cleanly. An offer that is contingent upon a buyer selling another property or obtaining mortgage financing sometimes falls through.

2. **Earnest Money Deposit.** To show the seller you're serious about buying the property, you must offer some *earnest money*, which you'll lose if you back out of the deal, unless you're backing out because of a contingency. A *contingency* clause (see No. 9 below) gives parties the right to back out of the contract under certain circumstances. A rule of thumb is the buyer will put down 1-2 percent of the sale price. But a buyer who puts down more and offers the same price and terms as another buyer would be in a preferred position.

3. **Real Estate Taxes and Adjustments.** This paragraph states that taxes and rents from current residents will be prorated at the time of the sale.

4. **Title.** This paragraph requires the seller to provide a legally clear *warranty deed* (title) to the buyer. This means that the seller is guaranteeing that he or she is the rightful property owner and has a legal right to transfer title. If problems develop, the seller takes responsibility.

> **Definition #18**
>
> *A warranty deed is a document in which the seller guarantees he or she has a legal right to transfer title to a buyer.*

5. **Possession of property.** This specifies the date on which the buyer will take possession.

6. **Risk of loss.** Until the sale, the seller assumes responsibility for all losses or damage to the property.

7. **Improvements and Fixtures.** Everything attached to the property or dwelling is transferred from the seller to the buyer, except that which is specifically excluded.

8. **General Conditions.** Both parties agree that the sales agreement is binding on heirs and representatives. This protects the parties

should one of them die or become incapacitated and unable to close the deal.

9. **Special Conditions.** The buyer (and, later, the seller) can add special conditions or contingencies. A *contingency clause* gives a party the right to back out of the contract if a condition is not met. A common contingency for buyers is to make the sale of the property contingent on a professional inspection. If the inspector finds major problems, such as mold or a broken sewer line, the buyer can back out without losing her earnest money.

10. **Time of Acceptance and Closing.** The buyer gives the seller a deadline for accepting the offer, and the sale will take place after the buyer is in possession of a title and/or title insurance that protects the buyer should a dispute emerge later about who owns the property.

You, the buyer, sign the contract and deliver it to the seller or their agent.

If the seller accepts the terms, they sign the contract. If not, the seller can make a counter-offer, to which the buyer then has a chance to respond. The negotiations can continue after this until both parties accept the agreement or one of them walks away.

> **Definition #19**
>
> *Due Diligence is a time period in which the buyer investigates the property's physical and financial condition.*

When you and the seller agree to terms, then *due diligence* begins—a period of time (usually several days to a week) in which you investigate the property's physical and financial condition (see a Due Diligence Checklist on the next page). Your home/building inspector will look for minor and major problems, and you can go back to the seller and ask them to correct the problems or provide financial compensation.

Text Box 7.2 – Due Diligence Checklist for a Rental Property

Exterior Inspection

Purpose: To evaluate all exterior components of the property and determine when they need repair or replacement.

Look for:
- Roof problems, including signs of leaks and overall disrepair or wear.
- The condition of heating, ventilation and cooling systems and the equipment service records.
- Electrical wiring that is not in compliance with current codes.
- Plumbing that is aged, corroded, or leaking and the type of plumbing: copper, PVC and galvanized all have their own unique problems.
- The condition of the exterior paint and trim.
- The condition of the driveways and parking lots. What repairs are necessary?
- Landscaping problems, including irrigation and sprinkler system breaks, large trees that need trimming, and root growth that is cracking sidewalks or causing foundation problems.
- Insect/pest problems, such as termites and cockroaches

Interior Inspection

Purpose: To help you learn about the physical property, get a sense of the quality of the renters (if they occupy a unit), and help you understand the exposure to your future cash flow should you purchase the property You'll determine the actual condition of the personal property and get a feel for the extent of major repairs.

Look for:
- Clues about the lifestyles of the current residents: drug activity; residents living without furniture, sleeping on the floor, and keeping articles in a plastic bag could be a future vacancy.
- Residents not living in units that the seller had designated as rented. Some sellers inflate their rent rolls or have such bad records that they don't know the current rental picture.
- Missing furniture, appliances, or items near the end of the useful life. Make a list of all appliances, carpet, vinyl floors and cabinets that fall into these categories.
- Major water, fire, or resident damage to the premises and contents
- telltale signs of pest problems in each unit and document any pest control needs.

Government Agency Reviews

Purpose: To determine that the property is in compliance with government standards.

Look for:
- Fire code violations. Invite the local fire department to complete an inspection.
- Outstanding permit problems. Have any remodels, additions, pools, and so forth been added without proper permitting?
- Environmental concerns such as asbestos, mold, lead paint, or radon gas.
- Zoning violations or encroachment onto another property.

Service Agreement Reviews

Purpose: To determine service commitments of the current owner and what you are responsible for.

Look for:
- Service agreements for pool, heating, air conditioning and cooling.
- Contracts for landscaping, coin-op laundry, cable TV, security alarm, parking, advertising.

The File Audit

Purpose: To verify the actual potential income of the property.

Look for:
- A signed rental agreement on every unit to ensure you have binding contracts.
- Monthly rental rates from the rent roll that match the numbers used in your offer.
- Security deposits should match escrow numbers; do residents pay their rent on time?

Insure Your Property

At the time of closing, you'll need to have an insurance policy to protect your investment, should it be destroyed by fire or storm. You'll also need liability insurance to protect you from injuries or death that may occur on your property. Landlords are sued more often than any other single type of business entity. And the more rental units you have, the greater the risk.

Insurance rates will vary greatly depending on the value of your property and whether you lease your property short term (at intervals less than six months) or long term (a minimum lease agreement of six months or more). For instance, John learned that if he rented his property on a long-term basis, the cost to insure his property would be $260 a year. But if he leased it short term, the cost was $1,090.

You may be tempted to lease your property without telling an insurance company that you are leasing it short term, but if there is claim, your company may not pay out. It's not worth the risk.

If no tenant is living in the property and you are leasing long term, your insurance company will issue a *vacant home policy* until the unit is rented.

A typical rental property insurance policy covers losses to the physical property and losses caused when people, either renters or visitors, are injured on your property. Damage from fire, lightening, explosion, smoke, riot, hailstorm, wind, and sprinkler/water pipe leakage are almost always covered. Damage caused by earthquakes and floods usually is not covered. You'll have to pay extra.

You can purchase insurance to cover actual cash value or replacement cost. The former means the company will replace or repair the damaged property less depreciation. The latter, which costs more, will replace or repair the full value of the property.

Liability insurance covers injuries people suffer on your property through accident or through the actions of someone else. So if someone slips on the ice on one of your sidewalks or is beaten up in a fight, you may be liable for injuries even though you did not cause the event.

Most landlords who purchase a home, condominium or town home will use higher liability limits than homeowners use ($1 million is common). Those limits are usually increased for a multi-unit property.

To reduce your risk of liability, keep your sidewalks clear during the winter and be sure your units meet or exceed building code standards. Fix problems immediately and listen to the concerns of tenants who identify problems in the units.

You can transfer liability for some problems to licensed and bonded contractors. If they fail to fix something properly and someone is injured, they will be partly or fully responsible. You should only do repairs and maintenance in areas in which you are competent.

John's Buying Experience

Properties in Sun City were selling like hot cakes when John finally got the money to purchase his rental property. Prices were increasing rapidly. John worried he wouldn't have enough money to buy a condominium, much less a single-family home.

But his real estate agent, who was a friend and not very familiar with properties in Sun City, referred him to an agent who had a lot of experience selling property there. Two weeks later, that agent found a two-bedroom, two-bath condominium property listed for $145,000, which was $5,000 more than John wanted to pay.

The kitchen and bathrooms and most of the flooring had been recently updated. The AC unit was only two years old. All of the windows had been recently replaced, with brand-new, high-quality, energy-efficient glass. No painting was necessary. The unit also included a washer and dryer and a carport with a storage unit.

The place was spotless. The seller kept the place well-maintained.

John knew almost the instant he set foot inside that this property was a good value.

But would the owner sell for $5,000 less?

John's new agent encouraged him to make an offer, because he was making a cash offer, which is much more attractive to most sellers. In addition, most sellers price their properties a little bit high to give themselves some wiggle room to go down.

The next day John learned there were two other offers on the place.

But the seller accepted his because it was in cash.

A home inspection revealed very few problems. John would have to do a little repair on the "built-up" roof, fix a toilet whose base was not securely fastened, and repair a kitchen vent fan. But that was it.

The seller also had a lot of furniture that she was going to leave behind if John wanted it. He agreed, although he hadn't planned on this.

The beds, kitchen table, and living room furniture were relatively new. She also gave him lamps, end tables, some dishes, coffee pot, pictures, wall hangings, pots, bed spreads, pillows, and synthetic plants.

John now had the option of renting the unit fully furnished.

Should he change his goals and turn it into a seasonal rental, which can generate more rental income per month than an annual rental?

There is more risk in a seasonal rental. People often book but then cancel at the last minute.

John also would have to pay electric and gas expenses. Short-term tenants are rarely responsible for such expenses. In the summer, the energy bills can top $150, but the amounts are usually half that or even lower in the winter.

John couldn't make up his mind.

He decided he would try to rent it on an annual lease. The furnishings would be optional for a small monthly fee.

He put a sign in the front yard (a modestly busy street) and posted the property at Zillow.

He got a lot of calls, often from people who were not fifty-five or older, which is a requirement to live in Sun City.

He also learned that $1,300 was a bit steep for most people. Many wanted to pay $1,000 or less.

Then one of the Zillow online inquirers wondered if she and her husband could rent it for three months, from December to February. They would pay $2,200 a month.

John said he would think about it and get back to them in two days.

He posted the property on Vacation Rentals by Owners, better known as VRBO (ver-bo). Customers can cancel without penalty thirty days before the start of the lease period. They only get 50 percent back if they cancel after that.

On the second day, someone rented it for March and April at $2,500 a month.

John changed his goals. He decided to convert it into a seasonal rental.

He accepted the offer from the other people to rent it from December to February. They signed a contract and put down a $1,000 earnest money check. If they didn't show, John could keep the money.

In the next three weeks, he leased three more months. One couple moved in immediately because they lost their home and were looking for a permanent apartment. By week five, John had leased the entire nine-month period with the exception of one week in November.

Wow. So let's look at the impact of John's decision to rent on a seasonal basis.

Evaluating John's Decision to Lease on a Seasonal Basis

Table 7.3 shows John's estimated expenses (taken from Table 7.1) with his actual expenses during the nine-month period.

Most of the items are the same or similar.

But his average monthly income increased substantially (from $1,300 to $1,956), his electric and gas bills increased from $8 to $73, and he had a new expense: Internet service and premium TV (Amazon Firestick). That turned out to be $82 a month. Long-term renters are expected to pay for internet and premium channels, but short term rentals almost always get those items at no charge.

The bottom line is that his cash flow tripled, going from $179 to $698 a month, which meant he earned a whopping $6,282 for the nine-month period compared with $1,611 under the estimated (annual lease) cash flow model.

Table 7.3 - John's Estimated and Actual Monthly Income and Expenses
(First Nine Months)

	Estimated	Actual
Income	$1,300	$1,956
Expenses	$1,121	$1,258
Cash Flow (Income - Expenses)	$179	$698
Total Profit for Nine Month Period (Cash Flow x 9)	$1,611	$6,282
Itemized Monthly Expenses		
1. Mortgage	$709	$709
2. Taxes	$41	$39
3. Insurance	$42	$22
4. Advertising	$2	$2
5. Annual recreation fee	$41	$41
6. Gas/Electric (when unit is unoccupied)	$8	$73
7. Water/sewer/garbage collection (covered by HOA fee in item 8)	$68	$0
8. Routine maintenance/repairs/landscaping (HOA fee includes water/sewer/trash/pest control/yard maintenance/painting/ landscaping/insurance)	$120	$200
9. Reserve/Contingency fund	$90	$90
10. Internet service and Amazon TV	$0	$82
Totals (Expenses)	$1,121	$1,258
Monthly Expenses Excluding Mortgage (Items 2-10)	$412	$549

Taking a conservative approach (that is, assuming John doesn't rent the property for the last three months of his first year of ownership,) and projecting these results to the next ten years, then John can expect to generate a cash flow of $76,479. This amount is more than three times greater than he would have earned had he leased the property through an annual contract.

So, when you add this additional cash flow onto the appreciation and principal payments in Table 7.4, John ends up with a total gain of $281,744 after ten years, which is $50,329 more than if he had rented the property on an annual basis. And the gains do not include any rental income during the summer months.

Shazam!

Table 7.4
John's Estimated and Actual Cash Flow
From His $140,000 Investment in 10 Years

Year	Estimated Cash Flow*	Actual Cash Flow**
1	$2,148	$6,282
2	$2,240	$6,552
3	$2,337	$6,834
4	$2,437	$7,127
5	$2,542	$7,434
6	$2,651	$7,754
7	$2,765	$8,087
8	$2,884	$8,435
9	$3,008	$8,798
10	$3,138	$9,176
Total Gains*** =	$26,150	$76,479

*Data extracted from Table 7.2. This is the total yearly cash flow estimated from renting the property on an annual contract.

**This is the actual cash flow for the first nine months on the property, which was rented on a seasonal basis. This figure doesn't include three additional months of possible income (May, June and July).

***These totals are adjusted for a 4.3% yearly increase in rent rates (the average increase in Sun City over the previous 10 years). See Table 7.2 for more details.

Chapter Eight

Step 5: Manage Your Property

Good people don't always make good business decisions.
Take some of my friends, for instance.

They owned a home and rented it out to a religious man who had a poor credit rating.

But my friends are kind-hearted, which normally is a good thing.

Except in this instance.

The renter's first check bounced.

He made some payments, usually late, and two years later he owed $15,000 in back rent. During that time, the renter also tore up much of the house, which eventually cost $55,000 to fix.

The lesson here is that *kindness is not a line item on a balance sheet.*

If you're going to be a successful landlord and property manager, you need to think like a business person, not a friend or social worker. Your relationships with tenants should be cordial but professional. Don't become too chummy, as some will assume you won't mind getting the rent check late or that you'll do them other financial favors.

I know this first hand.

My first job in real estate involved managing a sixty-unit apartment building in Seattle. Later, I managed a 600-unit community in Las Vegas. Many renters would ask me or the office staff to give them a break. But we had to decline.

> **Tip #23**
>
> *Your relations with tenants should be cordial but professional.*

Rules are rules.

The tenants were assessed late fees, which was enough incentive to deter most of them.

I want to emphasize that most tenants are good people and pay their rent on time.

But, as a landlord, you need to be ready for the outliers.

When a tenant fails to pay on time, you inform them—in person, in writing, or through a text or email message—that the lease requires you to assess them a small penalty (under law it normally can be no more than 5 percent of the monthly rent).

In this chapter, I'll show you how to be a good property manager. Alternatively, you should consider hiring a professional management company when your business becomes too big for you to handle by yourself.

Five Golden Rules of Property Management

Every experienced real estate rental property investor develops a set of rules to guide themselves. My list has five:

Rule 1: Maintain Your Property

After taking possession of your property, the first thing you need to do is fix the things listed on the home inspection report, especially those that might pose a safety or health problem.

If your unit is occupied, give notice immediately. This is an inconvenience to tenants, but most will appreciate your actions. They show that you care about the property and them as well. But even if they fail to see you as a caring person, keeping your property in good condition will reduce the potential of injury and lawsuits.

> **Tip #24**
>
> *A well-maintained property will reduce your risk to lawsuits.*

If your property is already in good shape, like John's, you won't have many repairs, but you probably will need to spray for pests like cockroaches, spiders, termites, and crickets. If a unit becomes infested, you can bet that other units around it quickly will become infested, and delays in treatment can cost you more down the road.

Most importantly, you need to create a schedule for replacing the batteries in smoke and carbon dioxide detectors. Don't assume your residents will do this, even if the lease says it's their responsibility. Safety is everyone's concern.

Some local or state jurisdictions require detectors to be electronically linked together, so that when one goes off, the others do, too. It's also a good idea to equip each unit with a fire extinguisher, although this sometimes is not required under state law. Check your state, city, or country regulations to ensure your units are in compliance.

Be especially diligent about water and electrical problems. An undetected leak in a pipe can produce unhealthy levels of mold, not to mention expensive damage to drywall and framing.

A broken electrical outlet is especially dangerous to young children. Encourage your tenants to call you immediately when something like this happens.

If you fail as a landlord to correct such conditions in a prompt manner and people are injured or are killed, you may be held civilly or criminally liable. Failure to respond promptly to a tenant's maintenance concern also is one of the biggest reasons residents cite for leaving a unit.

You should create a list of plumbers, electricians, and other professionals who can fix problems that you can't (such as air conditioning units or water heaters). Also, be sure to show your renters where to turn off the water supply to the house should a pipe break. That could save you thousands in repair costs.

When John took over his property, he fixed the toilet, the roof, and the vent. He also found a sink that was not draining well. Turned out there was a fair amount of crud (a kind word) in the pipe as it enters the wall for the journey down and into the street sewer system. A job like that could have cost him a couple of hundred dollars had he hired a plumber. He only had to spend $5 on new plastic piping.

But to get his property ready for seasonal leasing, John had to spend nearly $1,700 on furnishing the house, including dishes, pots and pans, a new TV and wall mount, a digital antenna, knick-knacks, blinds, coaxial cable, shower head, mattress topper, sheets, blankets, two dressers, and more.

Rule 2: ALWAYS Do Background Checks on Tenants

The single biggest fear rental property investors face are tenants who fail to pay rent.

Your best way to reduce this fear is to screen applicants.

Every prospective tenant must complete a *tenant background authorization application* (see Text Box 8.1).

The application should include information about the prospective tenant's finances, employment, and personal information. You should inform your applicant that the application gives you, the landlord, the authority to conduct a background check, which includes a criminal history report, a credit check, and phone calls or emails to past employers and references.

> **Tip #25**
>
> *A tenant background authorization application is your best tool for selecting good tenants.*

There are numerous sources online you can pay to conduct the criminal and credit background checks. Three of the most popular are TenantBackgroundSearch.com, MySmartMove.com and VerticalRent.com, all of which can give you a report for less than $50.

The cost of the background check, by the way, is usually borne by the tenant, but check your state law to make sure you can charge them. You might, being the nice person you are, apply the cost of the background check to the tenant's first month's rent.

Background checks are the single-most important way to deter problem renters. If convicted felons know you'll conduct a background check, they likely will not even submit an application.

In addition to making sure your tenants are law-abiding citizens and have a decent credit rating, you should check to see if they have a stable work history and have enough income to pay the rent. Can the tenant's income cover the rent plus normal living expenses? A general rule is that

Text Box 8.1 – Tenant Background Authorization Form

Fee for Background Check: $_____ Received By: _____
Telephone: _____ Property Address: _____
Rental Term: _____ Rent Amount: _____
(Additional occupants over 18 years old and Co-Signer must submit a separate application)

Name (First, Middle and Last Name): _____
Date of Birth: _____ Social Security Number (SSN): _____ Phone _____
Email: _____ Driver's License Number: _____ State: _____
Do You Have a Vehicle? ☐ Yes ☐ No If Yes: License Plate Number: _____ State: _____
Make: _____ Model: _____ Year: _____ Color: _____
Do you have any pets? _____ If yes, what type and size? _____

Additional Occupants List everyone who will be occupying the home
Full Name: _____ Relationship: _____
Full Name: _____ Relationship: _____
Full Name: _____ Relationship: _____

Present Address
Address: _____ Reason for Leaving: _____
Dates Occupied, From _____ to _____ Has Notice been Given?: ☐ Yes ☐ No
Rent Amount: $_____ Security Deposit Amount:$ _____
Landlord/Property Manager Name & Phone: _____

Previous Address(es)
Address: _____ Reason for Leaving: _____
Dates Occupied, From _____ to _____ Has Notice been Given?: ☐ Yes ☐ No
Rent Amount: $_____ Security Deposit Amount:$ _____
Landlord/Property Manager Name & Phone: _____

Current Income
☐ - Self-Employed - Attach Your Past 2 Tax Returns (Last 2 Years)   ☐ - Employed - Attach your last 2 Pay-Stubs
Employer's Name: _____ Supervisor's Name: _____
Phone:_____Ext._____ Your Position/Title: _____ Salary/Wage: $_____
Other Source of Income? ☐ - Yes ☐ - No If Yes, Describe: _____ Monthly Amount: $_____

Past Employment
Employer's Name: _____ Supervisor's Name: _____
Phone:_____Ext._____ Your Position/Title: _____ Salary/Wage: $_____

References
Contact Name: _____ Relationship: _____ Phone: _____
Contact Name: _____ Relationship: _____ Phone: _____
Contact Name: _____ Relationship: _____ Phone: _____

Authorization – Tenant Disclosure and Release

In connection with my tenant application with you, I understand that consumer reports which may contain public record information may be requested to evaluate my rental application. These reports may include the following types of information: names and dates of previous employers, public records, credit data, bankruptcy proceedings, eviction and criminal records, etc., from federal, state and other agencies which maintain such records. I hereby authorize procurement of consumer report(s). If approved as a tenant, this authorization shall remain on file and shall serve as ongoing authorization for you to procure consumer reports at any time during my contract period.

Signature: _____ Date: _____

Print Name: _____

the cost of rent should not exceed 30 percent of the resident's total income (or the total income of the number of wage earners who will live in the unit), or 40 percent for people with no debt.

The credit report also will allow you to assess how much of the remaining income goes to monthly minimum credit card and installment loan payments. If all of the debts add up to more than the monthly income, you know there's a problem.

Be sure to call previous landlords and references and confirm all of the information on the background form. Not all liars are bad credit risks, but bad credit risks often lie. Ask questions like these:

> *Does the tenant owe you any outstanding debt? Have a history of late payments? Caused any major damage in the rental unit? Disrupt the neighbors? Did the tenant receive his or her security deposit when moving out? Would you rent an apartment to this tenant in the future?*

Scrutinize the reasons the renters left other apartments and look for gaps in rental history. If the tenant had a difference of opinion with a previous landlord, don't automatically presume the tenant is wrong. Talk to the previous landlord and make your own assessment. Not all landlords are perfect, either.

John's first tenant planned to be there only six weeks, so John ran an informal online background check on the couple. They paid in advance and put down a security deposit, so he felt comfortable doing that. The couple that stayed from December through February paid the $6,600 fee in advance. All of his other tenants booked through VRBO and, thus, were pre-screened because they are required to pay in advance via credit card. Their addresses and phones are confirmed as well.

If you allow pets, make sure the renter's pet meets your criteria. Some communities or Homeowners Associations only allow small dogs. As a rule, large dogs don't fit well with apartment living. They need space to roam and exercise.

Review the background form before you start screening to make sure the tenant didn't exclude any information. Missing information could mean the tenant is hiding something.

Keep in mind as you review the credit history of the prospective tenant that almost everyone is late in paying a bill now and then. However, it generally is not a good idea to lease to people who have filed for bankruptcy (unless it stemmed from factors out of their control, such as medical expenses) or who have been sued for failing to pay back rent.

You may also want to ask the tenant to provide a paycheck stub to confirm their employment. Call the tenant's employer to confirm as well. They cannot give out salary details or other private information but they can tell you whether the tenant is a current employee.

If everything looks good, interview the tenant. Keep in mind, though, that the Fair Housing Act stipulates that landlords cannot discriminate based upon color, disability, family status, national origin, race, religion, or sex. You can face fines and punitive damages if you discriminate. Even worse, it's the wrong thing to do.

> **Fact #9**
>
> *The Fair Housing Act provides fines and monetary damages against landlords who discriminate.*

In addition, much of the information you gather on the background form is private, and you need to keep it confidential. State laws allow aggrieved citizens to sue for invasion of privacy.

When you finally find a good tenant, be sure to go over the details of the lease so he or she understands everything and can ask questions. The better the understanding, the fewer headaches you'll have later.

Rule 3. Use a Legally Valid Lease

A lease agreement spells out the responsibilities of both the tenant and landlord. In general, you're required to provide a safe and clean home for the tenant, and the tenant must treat the property with respect and pay you for living there.

> **Definition #20**
>
> *A lease agreement spells out the responsibilities of tenants and landlords.*

State and federal laws pertaining to lease agreements can be very complicated.

Fortunately, you don't have to learn all that stuff, nor do you need to write a lease agreement from scratch. Many state governments, real estate organizations, and private companies post sample lease agreements that comply with both state and federal law. You can usually obtain these free of charge. You can also pay a private online company to create one that is tailored specifically to your property.

To find a lease agreement, type "lease agreement for [insert your state]". Scroll down until you find a .gov site for your state. If you can't find a free sample lease for your state, then go ahead and purchase one. A $50 fee now could save you thousands of dollars later. You don't want to use an agreement that violates state or federal law. If you need an extra measure of legal security, see a real estate attorney.

Here are some of the major items you'll find in a lease (a sample page is also provided in Text Box 7.1 in Chapter 7):

Major Items in a Lease

1. **Property.** The location of the property to be leased.
2. **Term.** How long will the property be leased?
3. **Rent.** How much is the rent? If rent isn't paid on time, what's the penalty? How much do you charge when checks are returned for nonsufficient funds (NSF)? Your bank will charge you fees ranging from $25 to $40, so you need to cover these costs.
4. **Security Deposit.** How much security deposit is required and how it will be refunded? What kinds of deductions can be taken from the security deposit, such as late rent charges, unpaid utilities, cleaning, pet violation charges, unreturned keys, unauthorized locks, or fixture installations?
5. **Use of Premises.** Who is eligible to live in the premises? The names of everyone who lives there needs to be listed.
6. **Condition of Premises.** Tenant agrees the unit is safe, clean, and livable.
7. **Assignment and Sub-letting.** Tenant shall not sub-let without permission of the landlord.

8. **Alterations and Improvements.** The tenant shall make no alterations to building, such as painting, without permission of the landlord.

9. **Non-delivery of Possession.** The landlord is not liable should something out of his/her control make the premises unfit for living.

10. **Hazardous Materials.** The tenant shall not store hazardous materials on the property.

11. **Utilities.** Who is responsible for various utilities? Landlords often cover sewer, water, and trash pick-up. Tenants usually cover electricity and natural gas.

12. **Maintenance, Repair, and Rules.** Tenants are required to keep the property clean and safe.

13. **Damage to Premises.** This spells out what happens if the property is destroyed by fire or a storm and is uninhabitable.

14. **Access by Landlord.** Some states require landlords to notify tenants in advance when the former need access to the rental unit for repairs. As a landlord, you need to respect the privacy of the tenant. Under emergency conditions, landlords in all states can obtain access without tenant approval.

15. **Subordination of Lease.** If an entity such as a bank or government agency obtains control over the property and the landlord has no say in the process, the tenant's rights can be terminated.

16. **Animals.** This will specify whether animals are allowed and will require the tenant to comply with all laws and private covenants and agreements.

17. **Waterbeds.** Waterbeds are prohibited unless the landlord gives permission because leaks can do a lot of damage.

18. **Quiet Enjoyment.** A general statement that the tenant must respect the privacy of other residents living nearby.

19. **Indemnification.** The tenant agrees to reimburse the landlord for legal and other costs associated with violations of the lease or other agreements governing the rental unit.

A well-drafted lease is crucial for your protection.

Many leases are too short.

If it's not in the lease, it doesn't exist.

If your lease doesn't say anything about having pets, then you can't tell your renter to get rid of one. The leases for my properties are twenty pages long. That doesn't deter people from renting the property. They rarely read the lease. The purpose of a long lease is to spell out every possible event that might impact you and the tenant.

Tip #26

Be sure your lease agreement addresses everything: If something is not in the contract, it does not exist.

It is extremely important that you also abide by the lease. If you fail to do so, the tenant may bring a legal action against you. A court can fine you or in extreme cases even grant the tenant punitive damages, which are levied to punish landlords who violate lease agreements.

John downloaded a legally valid lease made available on the website of the Arizona Department of Housing. He made a few revisions, which included no smoking in the condominium (but outside patio is okay). He also included a clause for an earnest deposit, which short-term renters would forfeit if they backed out at the last moment (it's not easy finding another renter on short notice).

Rental Inspection Checklist

After the tenant signs the lease, you give them the keys and ask them to inspect the unit for damage before moving into it. Give them a Rental Inspection Checklist (a portion of a sample checklist is presented in Text Box 8.2), which they will use to record any damages they see in the unit. The resident is not responsible for paying damages on anything that was not in good working order when they moved in.

When the resident is finished, he or she should give the list to you. You should go over the items and make any repairs. You will note the fixes on the form. At the end of the lease, you'll then record on the Rental Inspection Checklist any damages the tenant made to the unit. You can then deduct from the security deposit the cost of repairing those damaged items.

Text Box 8.2
First Page of Rental Inspection Checklist

Rental Inspection Checklist

Complete this inventory checklist as soon as you sign the lease. Do not move anything into your apartment till after you have filled this out. Take pictures of any damages, dents, marks, etc... Have the apartment manager/landlord sign it as well. If your manager will not sign it send him/her a copy of it. You should keep the original copy for your records.

Living Room	Quantity/Specific Location	Condition on Arrival	Condition on Departure
Walls and Ceiling			
Floor Covering			
Windows (curtains, blinds, etc...)			
Doors			
Light Fixtures			
Lamp (s)			
Furniture (if applicable)			
Baseboards/Moldings			
Other			

Kitchen	Quantity/Specific Location	Condition on Arrival	Condition on Departure
Stove, Oven, Range, Hood, Broiler, Pans, Burners, etc...			
Floor Covering			
Windows (curtains, blinds, etc...)			
Doors			
Light Fixtures			
Cabinets/Drawers			
Counter Surfaces			
Sink, Gargage Disposal,			

Rule 4. Treat Tenants with Respect but Be Firm

It's wonderful to have good relations with your tenants.

But they need to understand your role and theirs.

Your job is to provide a safe and clean home and in return you receive compensation for your efforts. Their role is to respect the property and rules and pay their rent.

If your tenant fails to pay rent on time, you must impose a late fee, which generally is no more than 5 percent of the rent (state law governs fees like this). If they are frequently late, you don't have the authority to evict them as long as they keep paying the rent. But you can continue assessing late fees (only one per month) and deduct them from the security deposit when the lease expires.

> **Tip #27**
>
> *If your tenant fails to pay rent on time, you must impose a late fee to ensure they understand the contract must be enforced.*

When they fail to pay on time, you must call or visit them soon. If they aren't available, leave a message or a notice. They need to know you are on top of the issue.

Keep your relationship with your tenants on a professional level. Limit the time you spend socializing with them (unless you're leasing to a relative or close friend, of course). If your tenants think of you as a close friend, they might think you'll given them a break when they are unable to pay their rent.

Interacting with your residents is a big part of the job of property management. You must listen to their concerns and correct any problems as soon as possible. When the occasion arises, also remind them about the policies and rules.

If you own a multiple-unit property, you may have to deal with resident-to-resident issues from time to time. Disputes sometimes break out. Complaints about noise or loud music are common. You won't be able to solve these intra-resident disputes to the favor of both parties. You may be perceived as the "bad guy." But that's part of the job.

On occasion, one resident will ask you to evict another resident. This happened to me after one of my tenants (a husband) caught his wife sleeping with another resident. There was nothing I could do, of course, because the offending resident broke no lease rules or state law. You have to have a good reason to evict a tenant (see discussion later in this chapter).

I also recommend you keep logs of every communication with your tenants. Ideally, you should have them sign the logs as well, confirming the accuracy of the communication. This will save you headaches later when residents try to claim they didn't agree to something.

From time to time, you also will send your residents legal notices, such as breach of lease notices. Don't try to write your own notices. Many online sources provide samples of different types of notices that were composed by attorneys. Use them whenever you can, or hire an attorney to compose one.

One landlord who needed to spray for bugs failed to heed this advice and sent the following notice to his residents: "Notice to Bomb." The phones were ringing off the hook that day.

Rule 5. Respect and Enforce Tenant/Landlord Laws

Tenant/Landlord rules and laws apply not just to the tenant but to you, the landlord, as well. A court can hold you liable for failing to hold up your part.

You must provide a safe and clean dwelling. You must give the resident notice whenever you enter the unit, except in cases of emergencies. Consult the laws in your state to determine how much advance notice you must give.

When you respect the rules and laws, you set a good example for your renter.

How to Evict a Tenant

Evicting a tenant for nonpayment of rent or another reason is never a pleasant experience.

It consumes a lot of time and probably some costs you'll never recover.

But consider the alternative: A tenant who refuses to leave will drain your cash flow month after month.

You need a good reason to evict a tenant.

Here are five:

Five Legal Reasons to Evict a Tenant

1. *Nonpayment of Rent.* As you might expect, this is the most common reason for evicting tenants. The courts are highly sympathetic to landlords on this reason. But you generally cannot evict a renter

who piles up lots of late fees. As long as they pay the rent, they can stay.

2. *Lease Violation.* One of the most common lease violations is an unauthorized occupant or pet. Boyfriends and girlfriends of renters often move in without seeking permission from the landlord, but so-called "rogue tenants" pose liability problems for you. Same goes with pets, especially pets that have a history of problems. Unapproved subletting of the unit also violates most contracts. Most leases also prevent tenants from running businesses out of the units that involve retail traffic (home-based businesses that don't have customer traffic are exempted). Rental units are to be used for residential living only.

Nuisance complaints are another big reason for evicting tenants. If one of your tenants has a lot of loud parties, the police department can fine you, the landlord. You need to provide a formal (in writing) warning to the tenant, so that you have a record of warnings when you need to evict.

> **Fact #10**
>
> *Five valid reasons to evict a tenant include nonpayment of rent, lease violation, crime or drug-related activity, property damage, and expiration of lease.*

3. *Crime or Drug-Related Activity.* When one of your renters commits a crime, police and local government want to know about it. You can easily evict a resident who is selling or using drugs. Some states allow you to terminate a lease within twenty-four hours of receiving notice for crime-related activities.

4. *Property Damage.* It's not uncommon for people attending a rowdy party to damage a unit. Alcoholic beverages often take away inhibitions, sometimes prompting fights and displays of toughness.

If the tenant pays for the damage, you cannot evict them. But repeated cases of damage require you to expend a great deal of time and can be grounds for eviction.

5. *Expiration of Lease.* When the lease expires, the tenant is supposed to move out. Some don't and they stop paying rent. You can easily evict the squatter, because the tenant no longer has a right to occupy the dwelling.

The Formal Eviction Process

Each state has different procedures and rules for evicting tenants. Be sure to follow the procedures to the letter.

In most places, the formal eviction process involves about six steps:

1. *Notify the tenant in writing that you're terminating the lease for good cause. If the tenant refuses to leave, then you:*
2. *File an eviction action with the local court;*
3. *Gather your evidence for termination and attend a court hearing;*
4. *Wait for the court to issue an eviction notice;*
5. *Hire a sheriff's deputy, who shows up on eviction day and ensures the resident leaves peacefully;*
6. *Change the locks on the doors.*

If the tenant (defendant) fails to appear, the court will rule in your favor.

If you're thinking about turning off utilities or changing the locks without a court action, don't. It's not legal. Also, don't accept payment from your tenant if you have already filed for eviction, as this act can nullify the eviction process.

Part III

How to Manage Your Money

Chapter Nine

Step 6: Do Your Books

You purchased your first rental and spent several hundred dollars making improvements. Your first tenant gives you a check for the first month's rent and has moved in.

Now what?

Time to manage your money.

Bookkeeping is one task that few business people enjoy doing. You might also find it intimidating if you've never taken an accounting course.

But keeping track of your financial records need not be complicated.

In fact, all you need to do is keep your receipts and sort them into two piles: one for income (revenue) and one for expenditures (costs). Then, to obtain a ballpark figure of your cash flow or profit or to file your taxes at the end of the year, you simply deduct the expense total from your income total.

That's it.

No need to hire pricey accountants or purchase an expensive and complicated bookkeeping software program, many of which require you to pay a monthly fee of $20 to $100. (There are some inexpensive accounting programs that just charge a flat fee, but QuickBooks is the most widely used accounting system in the United States.)[38]

> **Tip #28**
>
> *Bookkeeping is very important. Don't ignore it.*

---

38 As of this writing, an online version of Quickbooks was available for $20 or month depending upon plan, and a non-online version was available for $299 (three-year license).

Whether you use a formal bookkeeping system is up to you. But managing your money is not optional when it comes to securing the future of your business. You'll need records to keep track of your profits, to pay your taxes, to obtain loans for additional property purchases, and to sell your property.

In this chapter, I'll introduce elementary accounting methods and terms and offer some tips on how to maximize your income and reduce your expenditures.

The Four Steps of Bookkeeping

Bookkeeping involves four basic steps:

1. Open a Business Checking Account
I covered this in Chapter 4.

As noted then, it's best to keep your personal financial affairs separate from your business or, at a minimum, keep good track of all expenses and income for your rental property business versus receipts for all other personal and business transactions.

If you need some credit to buy things for your property, apply for a credit card through your financial institution. If you're setting up a new business, the card may have to be issued in your good name until your business establishes some credit-worthiness. Some investment banks (such as BBVA Compass Bank in the United States) offer secured business credit cards.

2. Select an Accounting Method
You must choose one of two accounting methods, either *cash* or *accrual*.

Cash is the simpler method for small business owners. You record income when you receive it and expenses when you make a payment. At the end of the year, you report the two totals and other details to the IRS.

> **Fact #11**
>
> *Most small businesses use the cash method of accounting, which is simpler than the accrual method.*

The accrual method is more complex. You record income and expenses when you incur them, regardless of when you receive money or pay. This method means a company can show a profit for a year even though actual revenues are less than expenses.

Needless to say, when purchasing a rental property, you need to know which accounting method the seller used to calculate profits if your purchase decision is based on projected profits.

3. Select an Accounting System

As noted earlier, you don't need to hire an accountant or purchase an accounting software package if you only own a couple of rental properties. Just keep a pile of receipts for income and one for expenses.

But if your business is growing, you'll need to use an accounting software program or hire a bookkeeper or Certified Public Accountant to obtain loans or credit from financial institutions and to sell your properties.

Regardless of the accounting method and system you select, you'll have to deepen your understanding of accounting. Although the language of accounting can be complicated, you don't need to master everything to be an effective real estate investor. I've narrowed it down to twenty-one key terms, some of which are already familiar to you:

Accrued Expense: An expense that hasn't been paid.

Accounts Receivable: Sales or income (such as rent) that has not yet been collected.

Accounts Payable: Expenses that have not yet been paid.

Asset: Anything that has monetary value, from cash to land. The formula for calculating assets is as follows: *Assets = Liabilities + Equity*. If you purchase a rental property for $100,000 and put $25,000 down, your total asset is worth $100,000, because you have $25,000 in equity and $75,000 in liabilities. (See definitions for equity and liability below.)

Balance Sheet: A financial statement that reports assets, liabilities, and equity. Also called an *equity statement*.

Cash Flow: This is the inflow and outflow of cash in a business. A positive number indicates that more cash flowed in than out of the business. A positive cash flow usually means a profit, but it depends upon the time period under consideration.

Depreciation: The loss of value in an asset over time. An asset generally has to have substantial value to warrant depreciating it. Common depreciable assets include automobiles, air conditioning units, and rental buildings.

Equity: The value of a business or property after liabilities have been subtracted from assets *(Equity = Assets - Liabilities)*.

Expense: A cost incurred by a business.

Fixed Cost: A cost that doesn't change as a result of other conditions. For example, rent on a building that houses a business doesn't change if sales increase or decrease. The opposite of a fixed cost is a variable cost.

Income Statement: A financial statement showing revenues, expenses, and profits over a given time period. Also called a *profit and loss statement.*

Invoice: A bill that seeks payment from a person who owes your business money.

Liability: Debts to be paid. Common liabilities include accounts payable and loans *(Liabilities = Assets - Equity)*.

Liquidity: The speed at which something of value can be converted into cash. For example, stocks are more "liquid" than rental property, because you can sell stocks anytime but selling a property generally takes more time.

Net Income: The dollar amount earned in profits. Net income is calculated by taking revenue and subtracting all of the expenses in a given period (such as a month or year).

Net Margin: The percent amount reflecting the profit of a company in relation to its revenue. It's calculated by dividing net income by revenue for a given period.

Overhead: Expenses involved in running a business that do not include the making or delivering of the product or service. Overhead usually includes rent and salaries.

Profit: The financial benefit realized when revenue gained from a business activity exceeds expenses and taxes. Profit and net income are often used interchangeably.

Profit and Loss Statement: See "Income Statement."

Revenue: Sales or income earned in a given time period.

Variable Cost: Costs that change with the volume of sales (opposite of fixed costs). For example, if a company sells more of a product, it will need more raw materials in order to meet the demand.

4. Record Income and Expenses

After you decide your method and system of accounting, be sure to record your income and expenses. This allows you to: (a) monitor profits and growth of your business, (b) build financial statements, (c) keep track of deductibles, (d) prepare tax returns, (e) obtain loans, (f) sell your property.

Income

For rental properties, the IRS defines income as including any of the following: normal rent payments, advance rent payments, payments for canceling a lease, and expenses paid by the tenant.

Rental income generally excludes a security deposit if the taxpayer intends to return it to the tenant at the end of the lease. But if the taxpayer keeps part or all the deposit because the tenant doesn't live up to the terms of the lease, then the retained amount must be reported as income.

Tax Deductible Expenses

Expenses fall into one of two categories: (1) deductible and (2) depreciable.

Tax deductible expenses include things like interest payments on a mortgage, phone and utilities (portion used for business), transportation, entertainment expenses (most meals and entertainment expenses can only

> **Definition #21**
>
> *Tax deductible expenses include interest payment, utilities, supplies for repairs and maintenance, and use of vehicle.*

be deducted at 50 percent of their total value), supplies for repairs and maintenance (paint, drywall, plumbing, electrical, etc.), and use of vehicle.

Definition #22

Depreciable expenses include loan closing costs and remodeling expenses.

Always keep receipts for these purchases. You can use cash, but checks and credit or debit cards give you another record of the transaction. Using the same business credit card or bank account and keeping your personal purchases separate will make the accounting easier.

Depreciable Expenses

The following expenses must be depreciated: *start-up expenses* (your costs before you begin renting your property), remodeling projects (which add value to a rental property), and loan closing costs (which are part of the capital costs of a property).

Start-up expenses are those costs that occur before the day you list your property for rent. They include such things as the cost of travel and hotel when you're searching to buy a rental unit, and the costs of items you buy in advance to decorate or fix up your soon-to-be-purchased property.

Start-up costs are depreciated over fifteen years; however, the law gives new rental businesses a break: You can deduct up to $5,000. Anything over that amount must be depreciated.

So, if you spent $6,500 before listing your property for rent, you can immediately deduct $5,000 from your rental income—and the other $1,500 will be deducted over fifteen years, which means you only get to deduct $100 each year.

I'm sure you can see the lesson here: limit the amount you spend before the day you put your property up for rent, otherwise it will take years to recoup the expenses on your tax bill.

Remodeling expenses, just to be clear, do not include repairs to the property, such as fixing a leaking sink or replacing an electrical outlet. Those expenses can be fully deducted.

But when you remodel a kitchen or bathroom, you have to depreciate those costs over 27.5 years. So if the remodeling project costs $27,500, you can only deduct $1,000 a year from your income.

When it comes to loan closing costs on the property, you generally can only deduct home mortgage interest and annual real estate taxes. Other costs—such as abstract and recording fees, legal fees, title search and document preparation, land surveys, title insurance, transfer or stamp taxes, expenses you paid for the seller, points you paid to reduce the interest rate on your mortgage loan, easement payments, energy credits and energy subsidies—must be depreciated, usually over 27.5 years.[39]

Deducting Vehicle Expenses

Expenses for using a vehicle in your business also can be deducted. The rules are a bit more complicated, so let me explain.

In the United States, you have two options to write off expenses for your vehicle: *standard-mileage* and *actual expenses*.

In 2019, the standard-mileage option allows you to deduct fifty-eight cents from your business income for every mile you drive. (The IRS, by the way, has increased the deduction over time as inflation and the costs of repairing vehicles have increased.)

The alternative method for "writing off your vehicle" is the actual expense method, which involves deducting actual costs for maintaining a vehicle, such as gas and oil, repairs, tires, fees and taxes, loan interest, insurance, depreciation, and parking fees.

> **Fact #12**
>
> *The standard-mileage deduction for use of a vehicle for business is nearly 60 cents a mile.*

As a rule, the more economical your vehicle is to operate, the more likely the standard mileage rate will give you a bigger deduction. You are not restricted in the number of miles you drive and you can deduct the miles for as long as you own the car.

---

39 I highly recommend you read Tom Wheelwright's *Tax Free Wealth: How to Build Massive Wealth by Permanently Lowering Your Taxes*, Second Edition (Scottsdale, AZ: RDA Press, 2018) or Stephen Fishman's *Every Landlord's Tax Deduction Guide* (Berkeley, CA: Nolo, 2018).

But to use the expense method and depreciate your vehicle, you need to drive at least half of the miles for business use. If you don't drive that much, the standard-mileage method is the only option.

In either case, keep track of the miles you drive for business, including every trip to your rental properties, the bank, home supply stores, etc. You can use an app (many are out there) to record your mileage or simply record it in a book. You'll need to record five things: day, time, odometer reading start and finish, and purpose of trip.

If you want to use the actual expense method, keep all of your receipts. At the end of the year, you calculate what proportion of miles you spent driving for pleasure and for business and you get to deduct the percentage amount used for business. So, if a third of the miles you drove were for business, you get to deduct a third of the expenses for maintaining the vehicle.

If you're unsure which method gives you the best result, don't worry. Tax software programs will walk you through each approach step by step to determine which is most beneficial to you.

Set Up a Reserve or Contingency Fund

As in life in general, in business there are always unanticipated expenses.

Things break.

And when a big ticket item like an air conditioning unit goes bad, you could face thousands of dollars in expenses.

So I recommend that you set up a replacement reserve fund. Before you draw from your cash flow for personal use, put some money aside every month to prepare for that rainy day. You won't regret it.

Double-Entry Bookkeeping

Earlier I mentioned that bookkeeping can be as simple as creating two piles: one for your income and another for expenses.

This is called the *single-entry method of accounting*.

If you only have a couple of properties, you probably know at any single point in time whether your property is making or losing money. But if you own more properties, keeping track of the profitability of your business can be tricky, especially when you sell a unit in a year other than when it was purchased and when expenses and income are recorded in the year before or after the sale.

To rectify this problem, accountants have developed the *double entry method of accounting*. Each time an income or expense occurs, the balance sheet (also called equity statement or net worth statement) is updated immediately. Under the single- entry method, the balance sheet is often updated only once a year, at tax time.

> **Definition #23**
>
> *Double-entry accounting creates a balance sheet based on actual costs rather than market values.*

In double entry, the balance sheet is constructed based on actual costs rather than market values. So net worth increases or decreases as a result of profit or loss.

Are you confused?

Like I said, accounting can get complex.

My goal in this introductory book is not to teach you how to use double entry accounting (you can hire an accountant to do that for you), but to make you aware that if you intend to seek funding from investors or financial institutions, they will need to see your "books," and those books will have to use a double entry method. That's how these financiers are able to assess the profitability of your business.

Chapter Ten

Step 7: File Your Taxes

D id your blood pressure jump after reading this chapter title?
    If so, you're not alone.

More than half of all Americans tell pollsters that filing taxes is stressful.[40]

But it doesn't have to be that way.

If you keep good records, doing your taxes isn't difficult.

And the best part is that you don't have to hire an expensive accountant or tax attorney.

Free online software makes it easy to file both your personal and business taxes all in one program (https://apps.irs.gov/app/freeFile).[41] Alternatively, you can purchase for under $90 a tax software program, such as Turbo Tax (you'll need the "Home and Business" version).

All of these programs share one thing in common: They take you through the filing process step-by-step. All you do is answer the questions.

If your business is small and not too complicated, I recommend you do your own taxes, because you'll learn a lot about how the tax system operates.

---

40 Maruie Backman, "Most Americans Think Filing Taxes Is Stressful — But It Doesn't Have to Be," *The Motley Fool* (January 30, 2018), retrieved October 17, 2019, from https://www.fool.com/retirement/ 2018/01/30/most-americans-think-filing-taxes-is-stressful- but.aspx/

41 Note that these free tax programs are offered by private companies who may try to charge you for filing for state income tax return and sell you other services. High-income tax filers may not be eligible for the free software.

In this chapter, I'll explain how the tax system works for real estate investors, and then I'll show you how John did at tax time.

What Is Schedule E?

If you own and rent a property, you're required to file a tax return.

In the United States, the IRS requires you to file a Schedule E Form (Supplemental Income and Loss) along with your Form 1040 at the end of the year. You'll find Schedule E (Rent and Royalty Income and Expenses) under "Business Income and Expenses" in most online tax programs.

Are You a Real Estate Professional?

One of the first things the tax program does is determine whether you're a real estate professional, which means you must meet all three of these requirements:

1. More than half of the personal services you provided during the year were performed in a real property trade or business in which you *materially participated*—meaning you actually performed work on the property and were not just a *passive* recipient of income from it; and
2. The number of hours in which you materially participated in this real property trade or business exceeded 750 and you have records of this work; and
3. If you have more than one property, you materially (actively) participated in each rental real estate activity or you can file to group all rental real estate activities as one and participate in that grouped activity.

To simplify, if your full-time job is renting and maintaining rental properties, then you qualify as a real estate professional.

If you have a full-time job as a cab driver and just purchased your first rental property, you do NOT qualify as a real estate professional. (But

> **Fact #13**
>
> *Real estate professionals get a tax advantage: They can deduct losses from other income.*

don't worry, the tax law will be kind to you if you don't make a lot of money.)

If you have a part-time job, then it boils down to how much time you spend working that job versus your rentals, and whether you can meet the 750-hour requirement.

Why is all this important?

Real estate professionals get a tax advantage over *higher-income* nonprofessional investors.

If professionals incur losses in their rentals (which is very common because of depreciation and maintenance and mortgage interest costs), they can deduct those losses from income they receive from other sources (such as commissions from sales of homes).

Nonprofessionals cannot take such deductions if their yearly income exceeds $150,000 (modified adjusted gross income[42]). The maximum allowable deduction is the total rental income they receive.

So, if your rental earns $10,000 and your expenses are $12,000, you cannot deduct the $2,000 difference this year. But don't worry: You can carry that loss over to another year and deduct it when your income exceeds your expenses.

If, in the years that follow, your rental income never exceeds expenditures—which is possible on properties with low cash flow margins and high mortgage payments—then the carryovers will accumulate until the property is sold, at which time they can be deducted, reducing your capital gains taxes.[43]

In practice, the problem of expenses being greater than income is usually greatest in the year you purchase the property, because you often have to put extra money into repairs and maintenance and you have closing costs as depreciable and/or deductible expenses. The conventional

---

42 Modified adjusted gross income is the money you earn through wages, interests, dividends, rental and royalty income, capital gains, business income, farm income, unemployment, alimony, social security, tax-exempt interest, and foreign income and housing costs for qualified individuals—minus contributions to Individual Retirement Accounts, moving expenses, alimony paid, self-employment taxes and student loan interest.

43 When you buy properties, keep each as a separate business. If you pool your properties together under one LLC, you won't be able to take the carryover loss until you sell all of the properties.

wisdom is that you want to take as many deductions as you can now rather than later, because *a dollar today is worth more than a dollar tomorrow* (inflation makes dollars in the future less valuable).

Now, what happens if you earn less than $150,000, like John?

The law gives you a break, because it wants to encourage lower-income people like you and John to invest in real estate and climb the economic ladder.

If you earn less than $100,000, you get to deduct up to $25,000 in rental property losses from any other income you earn, such as a salary from a job or income from investments. If your losses exceed $25,000, you can carry them over to the next year or years thereafter until you sell your property.

If your income is between $100,000 and $150,000, the amount you can deduct is prorated and declines to zero as your income climbs to $150,000. But, fortunately, you get to carry over those losses to the next year and following years.

Your Property Profile

After asking whether you are a real estate professional, the tax program will ask you for information about the rental property: its address; when you purchased it; and whether the income you earned from it came from a 1099 tax form. Unless you're a *passive investor* in a real estate venture (such as giving your brother-in-law money to invest in a property and he, in turn, pays you interest in return), you won't receive a 1099 form, because your income comes directly from your tenants or renters.

Income and Expenditures

After providing profile information, the software asks you for the amount of rental income you earned.

Income includes rent payments from tenants, security deposits you have on file (when you give the deposits back they are recorded as an expense), repairs made by tenants in lieu of rent, and personal goods and services exchanged for rent.

You then provide a detailed list of costs and expenditures, including the amount you spent on advertising to find a tenant, travel (but don't include auto mileage, which is calculated separately), cleaning/maintenance (yard grooming, pest control, pool cleaning), commissions, insurance, professional fees, management fees, repairs, supplies, real estate taxes and other taxes, and utilities (gas, electric, water, sewer, garbage collection).

If you secured a mortgage to buy the property, you'll provide the lender's name and the amount of interest paid. The lender, by the way, will send you a 1098 tax form showing how much interest you paid on the mortgage loan during the year.

The program also will ask you to provide amounts for the abstract, legal, and recording fees; title search and document preparation; land survey; title insurance; transfer or stamp taxes; expenses you paid for the seller; points you paid to reduce the interest rate on your mortgage loan; easement payments, energy credits and energy subsidies.

Most of these closing costs must be depreciated. That means the costs (deductions) are spread out over 27.5 years. However, if you take out a loan on your personal home and use the proceeds for business purposes other than investing in another property, the closing costs can be fully deducted.

And, finally, there is a page in the tax software that allows you to list other expenses not included in those already mentioned.

Calculating Depreciation

The software automatically calculates depreciation for your rental property, which includes (1) the cost of the buildings and improvements; (2) closing costs associated with the purchase of the property; and (3), if you obtained a mortgage, the closing costs associated with that transaction.

As noted earlier, all buildings and improvements to the land (such as fences) are depreciated but not the land itself. The program will ask you for the price you paid for the property and the value of the land.

Some states or jurisdictions (like Arizona) don't provide separate values for the land and buildings on residential property. If the appraisal doesn't provide a breakout, you can generally use a 20-80 split rule (20 percent for the land and 80 percent for the improvements). However, if you have no appraisal and the land area is large relative to the buildings, then you should hire an appraiser to determine the split. If you don't, the IRS could send you a bill for taking too much depreciation.

The software also will ask you to list the amount you spent on remodeling, room additions, and special tax assessments (such as sewer line hookups). These expenditures must be depreciated over 27.5 years, too, because they add value to the property (also called *capital improvements*). Repairs just bring the property back to its useable condition and, thus, can be fully deducted in the year they occur.

If you obtained a mortgage loan on the rental property, most of the closing costs must be depreciated, as noted earlier. Points, which are prepaid interest, also must be depreciated over the life of the loan. In most cases, only taxes and mortgage interest paid during the year are fully deductible in that year.

> **Fact #14**
>
> *Section 179 of IRS rules allows large ticket items like refrigerators, computers, and stoves to be fully deducted in the year they are purchased.*

As noted earlier, start-up costs (usually those amounts over $5,000 that occurred before you purchased the property) are depreciated over fifteen years.

Other big purchase items—like refrigerators, stoves, washers, and dryers—also may be depreciated over time (the schedule varies by item, see Table 10.1). However, they also may be deducted. Under 2018 IRS rules (Section 179), items not fixed to the land can be fully deducted in the year they are purchased. Tax law allows small businesses to deduct up to $1 million.

The tax program will then calculate the total depreciation.

If you purchased after January 1, the program will prorate the depreciation. For example, if you purchased on July 1, which is halfway through the year, you'll get 50 percent of the depreciation for that year. Next year you'll get the full 100 percent.

Table 10.1
IRS Rental Property Depreciation Guidelines

1. Appliances, carpeting & furniture	5 years
2. Office furniture & equipment	7 years
3. Fences and roads	15 years
4. Residential rental buildings, structures, furnaces & water pipes	27.5 years
5. Commercial buildings	39 years

Note: The first two sets of items in the list also can be fully deducted under Section 179. The others must be deducted over the time periods shown.

1099 Form

When you hire people to do work related to your property, such as spraying for bugs or creating a lease document, they will invoice (or bill) you and you pay them. These workers are called *independent contractors*, because they control their work (use their own tools and supplies) and don't depend on you for benefits like a pension plan and insurance, as is the case for employees. Independent contractors, not you, are responsible for paying taxes on the money you paid them.

If the total amount you pay an independent contractor is less than $600 a year, all you need to do is keep the receipts and write them off as expenses. The contractor is responsible for reporting the income to the IRS.

But if you paid the contractor a total of $600 or more during the entire year, you're required to issue them a 1099 tax form (the form is easy to complete and comes with most home and business tax software programs), which reminds them of how much they need to

Fact #15

You will need to issue a 1099 form to any contractor to whom you pay more than $600 to in one year.

Text Box 10.1
W-9 Form – Request for Tax ID Number

Form **W-9** (Rev. October 2018) Department of the Treasury Internal Revenue Service	**Request for Taxpayer Identification Number and Certification** ▶ Go to *www.irs.gov/FormW9* for instructions and the latest information.	**Give Form to the requester. Do not send to the IRS.**

See Specific Instructions on page 3. · **Print or type.**

1 Name (as shown on your income tax return). Name is required on this line; do not leave this line blank.

2 Business name/disregarded entity name, if different from above

3 Check appropriate box for federal tax classification of the person whose name is entered on line 1. Check only **one** of the following seven boxes.

☐ Individual/sole proprietor or single-member LLC   ☐ C Corporation   ☐ S Corporation   ☐ Partnership   ☐ Trust/estate

☐ Limited liability company. Enter the tax classification (C=C corporation, S=S corporation, P=Partnership) ▶ _____

Note: Check the appropriate box in the line above for the tax classification of the single-member owner. Do not check LLC if the LLC is classified as a single-member LLC that is disregarded from the owner unless the owner of the LLC is another LLC that is **not** disregarded from the owner for U.S. federal tax purposes. Otherwise, a single-member LLC that is disregarded from the owner should check the appropriate box for the tax classification of its owner.

☐ Other (see instructions) ▶ _____

4 Exemptions (codes apply only to certain entities, not individuals; see instructions on page 3):

Exempt payee code (if any) _____

Exemption from FATCA reporting code (if any) _____

(Applies to accounts maintained outside the U.S.)

5 Address (number, street, and apt. or suite no.) See instructions.

6 City, state, and ZIP code

Requester's name and address (optional)

7 List account number(s) here (optional)

Part I   Taxpayer Identification Number (TIN)

Enter your TIN in the appropriate box. The TIN provided must match the name given on line 1 to avoid backup withholding. For individuals, this is generally your social security number (SSN). However, for a resident alien, sole proprietor, or disregarded entity, see the instructions for Part I, later. For other entities, it is your employer identification number (EIN). If you do not have a number, see *How to get a TIN*, later.

Note: If the account is in more than one name, see the instructions for line 1. Also see *What Name and Number To Give the Requester* for guidelines on whose number to enter.

Social security number

| | | | – | | | – | | | | |

or

Employer identification number

| | | – | | | | | | | |

Part II   Certification

Under penalties of perjury, I certify that:

1. The number shown on this form is my correct taxpayer identification number (or I am waiting for a number to be issued to me); and
2. I am not subject to backup withholding because: (a) I am exempt from backup withholding, or (b) I have not been notified by the Internal Revenue Service (IRS) that I am subject to backup withholding as a result of a failure to report all interest or dividends, or (c) the IRS has notified me that I am no longer subject to backup withholding; and
3. I am a U.S. citizen or other U.S. person (defined below); and
4. The FATCA code(s) entered on this form (if any) indicating that I am exempt from FATCA reporting is correct.

Certification instructions. You must cross out item 2 above if you have been notified by the IRS that you are currently subject to backup withholding because you have failed to report all interest and dividends on your tax return. For real estate transactions, item 2 does not apply. For mortgage interest paid, acquisition or abandonment of secured property, cancellation of debt, contributions to an individual retirement arrangement (IRA), and generally, payments other than interest and dividends, you are not required to sign the certification, but you must provide your correct TIN. See the instructions for Part II, later.

Sign Here | Signature of U.S. person ▶ | Date ▶

General Instructions

Section references are to the Internal Revenue Code unless otherwise noted.

Future developments. For the latest information about developments related to Form W-9 and its instructions, such as legislation enacted after they were published, go to *www.irs.gov/FormW9*.

Purpose of Form

An individual or entity (Form W-9 requester) who is required to file an information return with the IRS must obtain your correct taxpayer identification number (TIN) which may be your social security number (SSN), individual taxpayer identification number (ITIN), adoption taxpayer identification number (ATIN), or employer identification number (EIN), to report on an information return the amount paid to you, or other amount reportable on an information return. Examples of information returns include, but are not limited to, the following.

• Form 1099-INT (interest earned or paid)

• Form 1099-DIV (dividends, including those from stocks or mutual funds)

• Form 1099-MISC (various types of income, prizes, awards, or gross proceeds)

• Form 1099-B (stock or mutual fund sales and certain other transactions by brokers)

• Form 1099-S (proceeds from real estate transactions)

• Form 1099-K (merchant card and third party network transactions)

• Form 1098 (home mortgage interest), 1098-E (student loan interest), 1098-T (tuition)

• Form 1099-C (canceled debt)

• Form 1099-A (acquisition or abandonment of secured property)

Use Form W-9 only if you are a U.S. person (including a resident alien), to provide your correct TIN.

If you do not return Form W-9 to the requester with a TIN, you might be subject to backup withholding. See What is backup withholding, later.

Cat. No. 10231X   Form **W-9** (Rev. 10-2018)

report on their tax return. The IRS will go after them if they fail to report the income (and you if you fail to file the form).

At the time you hire independent contractors, you'll ask them to complete a W-9 form (see Text Box 10.1). The document is available at https://www.irs.gov/pub/irs-pdf/fw9pdf and requires them to provide you with an Employer Identification Number or a social security number and their address. As I'm sure you know, you must keep their social security number confidential. Under no circumstances should you give out those numbers, except to the IRS. If you can, keep them under lock and key.

Your contractor will sign the W-9 form and give it to you. You then use it to complete the 1099 forms, copies of which must be mailed to your contractors on or before January 31st. You also will send the IRS a 1099 form that includes a list of all the contractors and the amounts you paid them. As noted earlier, this report is easily generated by tax software programs.

If you have employees, you must withhold income tax, Social Security, and Medicare from wages paid and send these withholdings to the IRS. You most likely will need the assistance of a bookkeeper or accountant to do this.

The Home Office Deduction

If possible, you should set aside part of your residence for a "home office," because you can deduct that as an expense.

The tax software programs will guide you through the process.

Homeowners and renters can claim the deduction. You can use a freestanding structure on your property, such as a studio or garage, and you don't have to use the entire room or facility. But you must use that space exclusively for conducting business or for storing tools, inventory or materials related to your rental business. A bedroom cannot be used for both an office and playroom, unless you clearly divide the space.[44]

There are two ways to calculate the office deduction.

---

44 An exception is made for some business activities, such as caring for elderly or handicapped people in your home.

The simplest is to calculate the square footage of the space and multiply it by the IRS prescribed rate, which currently is $5 a square foot for up to 300 square feet.

The more difficult method involves adding up your overall residential expenses (electricity, natural gas, water and sewer usage, mortgage interest, maintenance, internet, insurance, and repairs) and deducting from your taxes an amount equivalent to the percentage of space your office occupies relative to your entire home or apartment. In other words, if your residential expenses for the entire year are $10,000 and your office takes up 10 percent of your home, your deduction is $1,000.

Regardless of which method you use, the tax software makes it easy to calculate your home office deduction. The actual expenses method just takes more time because you need to collect and keep all records of expenses.

Although the actual expenses method likely will produce more savings for you if you own a home, be aware that you might have to pay a capital gains tax when you sell your home. You are required to depreciate the value of your home, which means that if you use 10 percent of it for an office, 10 percent of your profit on the home's sale is now subject to capital gains tax.

The simplified method, in contrast, is not subject to such taxes, and may be the better choice for most new rental property investors.

Meals and Entertainment

Once upon a time, business people in America could party and entertain to their heart's content and deduct all of the costs.

Not so much anymore.

The IRS has removed many of the deductions for entertainment and some years ago knocked the meal deduction down to 50 percent. But you can still take a deduction for meals you consume while traveling for business and attempting to woo new clients.

To qualify for the deduction, the meal must meet four criteria:[45]

---

45 James Giacopelli, "How The New Tax Laws Affect Your Meals And Entertainment Deductions For 2018," *Forbes* New York Business Council (November 13, 2018), retrieved 10/20/2019 from https://www.forbes.com/sites/forbesnycouncil/2018/11/13/how-the-new-tax-laws-affect-your-meals-and-entertainment-deductions-for-2018/#30fb94e3606b/

1. *The meal must take place between you or your employee(s) and a current or prospective client.*
2. *The expense is incurred at a restaurant and not an entertainment venue such as a nightclub, cocktail lounge, or sports arena.*
3. *The meal is not lavish or extravagant under the circumstances.*
4. *There's a reasonable expectation of deriving income or other business benefit from the meeting.*

Be aware that taking large deductions for meals will enhance your chances of an IRS audit.

John's Tax Bill Estimate

As promised at the beginning of this chapter, it's now time to do John's taxes on his rental.

Recall that he purchased a $140,000 condo in Sun City and turned it into a seasonal rental.

Let's do his first year taxes, to see how he fares.[46]

First, we have to ask four questions:

1. Is he a real estate professional?

To begin, John doesn't qualify as a real estate professional, but that doesn't matter much to him, because his income is well below $100,000 a year and, thus, he qualifies for the $25,000 deduction rule. That means if he loses money on his property, he can deduct his losses from his other income. Otherwise, he'd have to carry over his losses into future years, when his income exceeded his expenses (or when he sold the property).

2. Is he an active investor?

John qualifies as an active real estate investor, because he is managing his property. He is not a passive investor—a person who basically gives his money to others who then purchase a property and pay him back with interest.

---

46 To simplify the analysis, we'll assume he purchased the property on January 1.

Passive investors face limits on the amount of deductions they can take. For example, an investor who takes out a loan on his house and uses the money to invest in someone else's real estate project cannot deduct the interest on that loan. He can only deduct that interest if he is an active investor.[47]

3. What is the value of his property?

Arizona assessed property valuations for homes don't separate the land from the improvements.

So, using the 20-80 rule, the value of the land on John's property is $28,000 and his rental unit is valued at $112,000. So the depreciation for his property will be based on this latter figure.

4. Did he earn income on his property?

He did, of course.

But if he was unable to find a renter, any costs he incurred would have to be depreciated, not deducted. The IRS will not allow real estate rental property investors to deduct expenses unless their property generates some income.

Now let's look at John's income and expenses.

I've broken down John's income and expenses into nine major categories: (A) rental income, (B) depreciation on his rental home, (C) depreciable closing costs on his rental, (D) deductible closing costs on his rental, (E) depreciable closing costs on his cash-out refinance mortgage, (F) mortgage interest, (G) repairs and maintenance, (H) mileage and auto insurance deductions and (I) home office deduction. All of these items are summarized in Table 10.2 at the end of this chapter.

A. Rental Income

Table 7.3 in Chapter 7 shows the actual income and expenses John incurred on the property, mostly broken down per month. We'll multiply most of those amounts by twelve, except with respect to income.

---

47 See "What Are Deductible Investment Interest Expenses?" Turbotax, retrieved 10/15/2019 from https://turbotax.intuit.com/tax-tips/investments-and-taxes/what-are-deductible-investment- interest-expenses/L9TeFQAf9

He decided at the last minute to rent it as a seasonal, which generated $1,956 a month in fall, winter and spring months (peak season). No one rented it during the three months of summer, because it's hot in Phoenix and few visitors come to town.

So his total income from the property is $17,604.

B. Depreciation on Rental Home

Depreciation is calculated using the following formula, where 27.5 represents the total number of years a property can be depreciated under tax rules and the land is worth 20 percent of the total cost of the property:

$$\frac{\text{Value of the property excluding land}}{27.5} = \frac{\$112,000 \ (80\% \text{ of } \$140,000)}{27.5} = \$4,073 \text{ per year}$$

So John gets to deduct $4,073 from his rental income every year for the next twenty-seven years, and in the twenty-eighth year he gets to deduct about half that amount.[48]

C. Depreciable Closing Costs on Rental Home

John will be able to deduct or depreciate two sets of closing costs. The first pertains to his rental property and the second to his cash-out refinance mortgage.

Some of the closing costs on the rental home must be depreciated, because the IRS considers them to be capital improvements and one-time costs. This includes escrow fees, HOA transfer fees, a one-time Sun City preservation fee ($3,500), a recreational center transfer fee, and a document fee.

The total amount of the depreciation is $4,681, which means John can only take a deduction equal to about 1/27.5 of that amount, or roughly $170 this year. But he gets to take that deduction for the next 26.5 years.

---

48 Note that the first year of depreciation is slightly less than $4,073, because the IRS calculates the amount using 11.5 rather than 12 months. The missing one-half month is made up at the end of the 27.5 years, when the deduction is 6.5 months.

D. Deductible Closing Costs on Rental Home

The second set of fees on the closing of his rental property can be fully deducted. This includes the one-year home warranty, annual recreation fee, HOA fees (two months paid in advance) and real estate taxes. These costs are recurring expenses and not associated with capital improvements.

The total comes to $1,437, but three of these costs (annual recreation fee, taxes, and monthly HOA fees) are included in the repairs and maintenance cost estimate (in Table 7.3 and under H in Table 10.2).

John and the seller split the cost of the home warranty fee, which came to $250.

E. Depreciable Closing Costs on the Refinance Mortgage Loan

John can fully depreciate the cost of the underwriting fee (or origination fees), points, appraisal fee, credit report, service fees, closing fees, document fees, deed prep fee, and title insurance on his refinance mortgage. However, if he were using the funds to make purchases for business, as opposed to investing in a property, he can fully deduct the costs.

John cannot deduct the taxes or insurance premium payments because those costs are associated with his personal property, not with his rental property. But he can depreciate the points, because that "fee" is a business cost (it reduced the interest rate on his loan by a quarter of a percent).

The depreciable costs on John's refinance mortgage came to $2,136.

F. Mortgage Interest

With a 4.5 percent mortgage rate, John paid $709 a month in interest and principal on his mortgage. As noted earlier in this book, about $188 a month went to principal. The rest, $521, went to interest.

That comes to a $6,252 interest deduction for the entire year.

G. Expenses for Maintenance and Repairs

John's monthly expenses for maintenance and repair (excluding mortgage interest and principal payments) came to $549 a month, or $6,588 for the year (see Table 7.3). This includes taxes, insurance, advertising, annual recreation fee, gas/electric costs, routine maintenance and repair costs, reserve/contingency fund, and internet service and Amazon TV.

H. Mileage and Auto Insurance Deductions

During the year, John drove 900 miles going back and forth between his home and his rental property, which was located about twenty-two miles from his home. So his deduction is 900 x .58 cents per miles, or $522.

He also was able to write off 10 percent of his $800 auto insurance premium (or $80), because he drove a total of about 9,000 miles during the year (9,000 miles ÷ 900 miles).

I. Home Office and Meal and Entertainment Deductions

He also set up a home office to use exclusively for his business.

It is 100 square feet, so he gets a $500 tax deduction ($5 per square foot x 100).

He could have taken a bigger deduction had he added up all of his utility, maintenance and repair expenses for his home and then multiplied those expenses by 5 percent. But when he sold the home, he would have to pay capital gains taxes on 5 percent of the profits.

John did not take a deduction for meals or entertainment, because he didn't entertain any of his renters in an attempt to get them to lease his property.

Table 10.2
John's Tax Bill for Schedule E

	Annual	Monthly
A. Total Rental Income	$17,604	$1,467
B. Depreciation on Rental Home in Sun City ($112,000 ÷ 27.5)	$4,073	$339
C. Depreciation for Closing Costs on Rental ($4,681 ÷ 27.5)*	$170	$14
D. Deductible Closing Costs on Rental Home**	$250	$21
E. Deductible Costs on Refi Mortgage on John's House***	$2,136	$178
F. Mortgage Interest	$6,252	$521
G. Repairs & Maintenance (includes property taxes)****	$6,588	$549
H. Mileage and Auto Insurance Deduction	$602	$51
I. Home Office Deduction (100 square feet x $5)	$500	$42
J. Total Deductions (B+ C + D + E + F + G + H + I)	$20,571	$1,714
K. Total Income Reported on Tax Bill (A – J)	–$2,967	–$247

*Depreciable closing costs include points, underwriting fee, appraisal fee, credit report, service fees, flood certificate, title and escrow fees, deed prep fees, one-time recreational fees. These items varied for the
**Home warranty
***Includes all closing costs but not home insurance or taxes.
****This includes taxes, monthly HOA fees, utilities and all repair and maintenance costs
Note that some totals may be off slightly because of rounding errors

John's Tax Bill Calculated

Table 10.2 shows a summary of his tax bill.

His total annual income from the property was $17,604.

His total expenses, including direct expenses and depreciated expenses, came to $18,506.

His total tax bill for the rental property is -$902, which means he gets to deduct this amount from other income he earned.

But this isn't a real loss.

His property actually generated $19,181 in equity during his first year. This included $10,640 in appreciation, $6,282 in cash flow, and $2,259 in principal payments (see Tables 7.2 and 7.4).

The deduction saved him about 20 percent on his taxes, or an additional $180.

Needless to say, John moved quickly to purchase his next property.

How to grow your wealth is the next topic of this book.

Part IV

How to Grow Your Wealth

Chapter Eleven

Step 8: Boost Revenues and Cut Costs

Time to take a deep breath and reflect.

Despite the odds, you cobbled some funds together and purchased your first rental property. You fixed it up and found a tenant and are depositing rent checks in the bank and paying off the mortgage.

You're not rich yet, of course, but you've taken the first big step down the path of financial independence.

So what's next?

Another property purchase, of course.

But you don't have equity for a down payment, because you poured everything into the property you just purchased.

And that's a good thing.

Because that's where you'll get much of the money for your next purchase.

You're going to leverage your rental property.

It might take a few years—until appreciation, cash flow, and principal payments build some equity. When I purchase apartment complexes, I normally refinance the property in three to eight years. I pay off investors and

> **Tip #29**
>
> *Consider refinancing your rental properties in three to eight years, when enough equity has accumulated.*

take a little for myself—tax-free, of course, because the funds are equity, not income.

I'll talk more about how to buy your next property in the next chapter.

Meanwhile, while you're waiting for equity to build, there are other things you can do to enhance the value of your investment.

One is to increase your rental rates. Another is to reduce your costs.

Increasing Your Rental Rates

None of the landlords I know enjoy increasing rents on their residents, especially if they are retirees on fixed incomes.

But the costs of repairing, maintaining, and insuring a rental unit are always increasing, partly because of

(1) inflation and market downturns (insurance rates, for example, increase when the market declines, because insurance companies have to make up for lost investment revenue),

(2) governmental regulations (like new safety regulations), and

(3) reduced competition in the do-it-yourself hardware market (the two big box chains now control nearly 50 percent of the market).

Maybe not now, but at some point you're going to have to increase the rent to keep pace with increasing costs.

History of Rental Rates

The history of rental rates shows that they have risen faster than the rate of inflation.

Since 1980, the monthly median asking rent for unfurnished apartments has increased an average of 4.4 percent per year, versus 3 percent for inflation.[49] This even takes into account the fact that rents were flat between 2007 and 2012, when the housing market and

> **Fact #16**
>
> *Historically, rent rates have risen faster than the rate of inflation.*

---

49 Rent statistics obtained from Statistica, retrieved October 17, 2019, from https://www.statista.com/ statistics/200223/median-apartment-rent-in-the-us-since-1980, and inflation statistics obtained from Official Data Foundation, http://www.in2013dollars.com/1980-dollars-in-2017?amount=100/

the economy were in crisis. Since 2012, rents have increased at an average of 6.5 percent per year.

The U.S. government recommends that renters only spend about 30 percent of their income on rent. But baby boomers are spending about 36 percent and millennials are spending more than 40 percent. The figures have been increasing because income has not kept pace with housing costs.

Rental rates are sensitive to inflation, but they also respond to the supply and demand for housing, mortgage rates, market conditions, and the cost/benefits of losing a tenant.

Demand for Housing and Mortgage Rates

If a major corporation decides to employ thousands of workers in a city, rental rates and housing prices near the facility are likely to increase, because demand for housing increases.

When mortgage rates increase, rental rates also tend to increase. That's because the high cost of buying a home prevents some renters

> **Fact #17**
>
> *Rent rates tend to increase as mortgage rates increase.*

from entering the housing market, which in turn drives up demand for apartments.

Market Conditions

Your ability to raise rental rates will depend upon the market in which your property is located.

Rents tend to go up more quickly in big cities, where demand for housing is higher and jobs are plentiful. This applies especially to San Francisco, Washington D.C., New York City, Boston, and Los Angeles. All of these cities experienced rent increases of 50 percent or more from 1980 to 2014, even when adjusting for inflation.[50] And in those cities, rent increases outpaced increases in income.

Phoenix, Las Vegas, and Austin are the only major cities where income has kept pace with rent increases. Rents increased slower in Phoenix and Las Vegas (less than 15 percent from 1980 to 2014), whereas in Austin

---

50 Data for this section are drawn from Apartmentlist.com, retrieved 10/20/2019 from www.apartmentlist.com/rentonomics/rent-growth-since-1960/

rents increased more than 40 percent. Since 2014, however, rents in Phoenix have risen more sharply (about 8 percent a year).

Rental rates have increased substantially in many cities in the South and Midwest even though wages have been stagnant. In other big cities, including Atlanta, Salt Lake City, Denver, Seattle, Tampa, and Orlando, rents increased but incomes also rose. To find the rates in your city, visit ApartmentList.com, which contains a wealth of information about rental rates and tenants, including renter satisfaction data.

The upshot is that your ability to raise rents will vary from market to market and from overall economic conditions, including the cost of borrowing money. You must carefully examine your market before raising your rental rates. You don't want to price your unit out of the market but you need to keep up with rising costs.

Cost/Benefits of Losing a Tenant

The general rule in the rental business is that you shouldn't raise rents by more than 5 percent on residents who are living in your units.[51] Increases greater than that are one of the biggest reasons residents leave to find other accommodations.[52]

And when residents leave, your costs generally increase.

That's because you probably will have to clean and possibly repair the apartment and place advertisements to get another tenant, and you'll lose some rent because your unit will be vacant, perhaps up to a month or more (many people like to move in on the first of the month).

Before raising your rent, it's useful to run a simple *cost/benefit analysis* to see how long it will take to recover your losses.

Let's assume your apartment rents for $1,000 a month. If you raise the rent 5 percent, the monthly rent increases to $1,050, so you'll collect $600 more a year. But if your tenant moves out, you may lose a month of rent, not to mention incurring other costs (like advertising and repairs).

---

51 This concern doesn't exist for vacant units. Just make sure you aren't pricing your unit out of the market.

52 Sterling White, "The 5 Most Common Reasons Tenants Leave Your Rentals," BiggerPockets, retrieved 10/20/2019 from www.biggerpockets.com/blog/reasons-tenants-leave/

So in this example, it will take about two years to recover that $1,000+ loss.

Is it worth it?

Some landlords never raise rents on current residents because they don't see the benefits as exceeding the costs. But after a decade or so, the value of your rental income will drop significantly because of inflation. In fact, a dollar in 2009 was only worth 80 cents in 2019 (20 percent less).

Another option that represents a compromise is to raise your rents very slowly, like one to three percent a year.

At the end of ten years, how much difference would a small increase like 2 percent make?

The answer is a lot.

Table 11.1 shows that a landlord who didn't raise rates earned $12,000 a year in rental income ($1,000 a month x 12), or $120,000 after ten years.

Table 11.1
Yearly Cost/Benefit Analysis of Raising Rent Over 10 Years
$1,000 Monthly Rent, No Increase vs. 2%

Year	No Increase		2% Increase Per Year	
	Yearly	Cumulative	Yearly	Cumulative
1	$12,000	$12,000	$12,240	$12,240
2	$12,000	$24,000	$12,732	$24,972
3	$12,000	$36,000	$13,512	$38,484
4	$12,000	$48,000	$14,628	$53,112
5	$12,000	$60,000	$16,152	$69,264
6	$12,000	$72,000	$18,192	$87,456
7	$12,000	$84,000	$20,892	$108,348
8	$12,000	$96,000	$24,480	$132,828
9	$12,000	$108,000	$29,256	$162,084
10	$12,000	**$120,000**	$35,664	**$197,748**

The other landlord raised rates 2 percent per year (compounded), which meant he took in $12,240 after the first year, and by the tenth year, he is taking in $35,664 a year—nearly three times as much as the first landlord.

> **Tip #30**
>
> *Small increases in rent can amount to a lot of revenue over time.*

At the end of the tenth year, the rent-raiser earned a total of $197,748 in rental income, compared with $120,000 for the landlord who didn't raise rents.

Now imagine the differences after twenty years and if the numbers were adjusted to reflect the average annual rent increase of 5 percent, instead of 2 percent. This is just another indicator showing why people who invest in real estate often become some of the wealthiest people in their communities.

How to Reduce Costs

If you can't raise rent rates to keep pace with inflation, then try to decrease costs.

You can start this process by looking at a list of expenses on your property.

1. Your Mortgage or Equity Loan Rate

Is it too high? Can you convert your equity loan into a conventional mortgage, which normally should decrease your interest rate?

Check to see if the monthly payment is lower even though you have to pay for closing costs. If so, that might be a good option if you plan to hold on to the property for at least five years (a general rule of thumb when it comes to paying closing costs and points).

2. Taxes

Is your property being overtaxed?

You can check this at Zillow by looking at the values of homes located around your rental property and checking the tax records of your home compared to the others.

If your property is paying 20 percent more than others that recently sold, you might file an appeal with the property tax assessing authority.

You lose nothing if the authority rules against you.

3. Insurance

Home insurance rates can vary greatly from company to company.

It's easy to get new quotes.

If you don't want to do the legwork, contact an independent insurance agent, who can search scores of companies to find you the least expensive option.

Be sure your property isn't over-covered—and that you are not paying for more coverage than you need.

4. Advertising

Have you tried putting a for-rent sign on your property when it becomes vacant?

That is often a lot cheaper than placing advertisements in news media or social media.

John's property was located on a moderately busy street, and he found that he received more calls from prospective residents who saw the sign than from ads he had placed.

5. Homeowners Fees

If you have to pay HOA fees for your property, there often isn't much you can do to reduce the fees.

But, depending on your HOA rules, you might join or seek election to the HOA management board, where you might be able to find ways to reduce costs for everyone in the housing community, such as getting multiple bids when the time comes to hiring a lawn maintenance/landscaping firm.

6. Gas/Electric and Other Utilities

If your tenant pays the gas and electric bill, you may not concern yourself with such costs.

There also isn't much any of us can do to reduce rates from utility companies.

But if you pay those costs, you might consider adding insulation in the attic or around piping. You should do a cost/benefit analysis, however, especially if you don't intend to keep the property for a long time.

7. Routine Maintenance and Repair Costs

When you have to contract with vendors to do repairs on your property, always get more than one bid.

The rates that electricians, plumbers, painters, tilers, and others charge vary greatly.

Of course, to really save money, do the work yourself if you are competent. You might also be able to hire friends or neighbors to do jobs that don't require technical knowledge (like raking leaves, picking up trash, cleaning up areas).

8. Internet Service and TV Programming

The costs of internet service and television programming have become more competitive in recent years, especially with the advance of streaming channels.

Search around for the best price but be aware that some forms of internet delivery are faster than others. Speed is often a big concern among residents.

9. Accounting and Taxes

If you can, do your own books and taxes.

It will save you a lot of money.

But if you have a question, seek out expert advice. Sometimes the experts can save you a lot of money or keep you out of legal and tax trouble.

Above all, always follow the law.

Chapter Twelve

Step 9: Build Your Rental Portfolio

You've watched your rental property appreciate in value, and you've done as much as you can to increase revenues and decrease costs.

You now have some equity.

And you know what you can do with it.

Buy another rental.

You're going to use the equity from your previous rental purchases because this gives you a maximum deduction at tax time. You get to deduct or depreciate a lot of closing costs that you normally would not get.

Okay, so you now know how you're going to fund the next purchase.

But you're nervous.

Can I make the mortgage payments on two properties if something goes wrong—like losing my day job or failing to find a tenant for my properties for extended periods of time?

Doubts like these are common.

John had them before purchasing his second property. And I confess I still get a few butterflies whenever I purchase or build an expensive apartment community.

Real estate investing, like all forms of business, has its risks.

But you know now how to reduce those risks.

Research.

The more information and knowledge you generate about the market, the rental property, and your financial condition, the more secure you'll feel in buying your next property.

You need to figure out how much you can afford and then stay within that limit, even when your real estate agent is advising you that "this property is a helluva good buy."

Purchase only when you feel confident your risks are minimized.

That's what John did.

John's Second Rental Purchase

Recall that John, after purchasing his first rental property in Sun City, leased it on a seasonal rather than year-round basis.

This initially posed some risk, as he worried about whether the condominium would be booked continually through the peak fall, winter, and spring months.

Fortunately, the property was leased very quickly and it generated a higher cash flow than what he would have received had he rented it year-round.

Now he was ready to buy a second rental property.

Should he lease that as a seasonal as well?

Reducing Your Risk

Although a seasonal rental can generate more profits, it also needs to be furnished, and that can be costly. If he turned his second rental property purchase into a seasonal, John estimated he would have to spend as much as $2,500 on bedding, furniture, dishes, and other household goods.

He had an advantage on his first rental, because the seller left a lot of furniture behind. Nevertheless, it still cost him about $1,700 to furnish the place. He had to buy dishes, pots and pans, silverware, sheets, blankets, pillows, mattress toppers, rugs, towels, cleaning materials, a new television, a rooftop broadcast TV antenna, and internet service.

With two seasonal properties, he also worried about what would happen if the state or nation slipped into a recession and the demand for seasonals dropped dramatically. When times are tough, people cut discretionary spending first.

John decided to spread his risk.

He would turn his next purchase into a year-round rental.

That way he didn't have to spend a lot of extra money to furnish the place. Nor did he have to clean it every time a tenant left. He could, at a future time, turn it into a seasonal if he wished.

He felt more confident about his next purchase.

Like John, you should carefully weigh all of the options facing you before you purchase your next property. Spread your risk whenever you can.

Show Me the Money

John wanted to put as little down as possible on the next purchase, but he learned after talking with lending experts that his income wasn't high enough to cover the purchase.

As a rule, most mortgage companies require your mortgage payments to be no more than 45 percent of your income if you have excellent credit. And, unfortunately, they will not allow rental property buyers to count the rental income they receive from the property they are purchasing. They use only the income you earn up to the present.

Although John's first property had generated $17,604 in rental income (see Table 10.2), all of this income was offset with losses. In fact, John showed a $902 loss.

So, to secure the loan to purchase his next property, John had to use all of the equity in his rental property, which was $140,000. But that still wasn't enough. Most mainstream lenders require you to show more income to purchase another property. John didn't have the extra income. So he had to find a private lender.

John was caught in what is called a "Catch-22."

A Catch-22

The term Catch-22 comes from the Joseph Heller book of the same name, and refers to a dilemma in which there is no escape because of mutually conflicting conditions.

Let me illustrate with John's situation.

To purchase his first rental property, John had to show that he had enough income to make the mortgage payments even though the entire loan was collateralized by his home, which he owned outright. In determining his income, the lending institution would not let John use the rental income he expected from the property. But his retirement and part-time work income qualified him for the loan.

He now owned, free and clear, a $140,000 rental home in Sun City. But to purchase his next home, the bank required him to report a higher income. Although he was now drawing rental income, his total income actually declined because he now could write-off thousands of dollars in depreciation, repair and maintenance costs, and closing costs for the loan and property purchase.

Although he could use the entire rental property as collateral to get his next loan, his bank would not give him a loan because his income had not increased enough to cover the mortgage payments on the second loan.

Catch-22.

He can't earn more income without obtaining more rental properties but he can't buy more rentals because he doesn't have enough income. So how did he resolve this dilemma?

He had two options.

He could take on a few more part-time consulting jobs to boost his income. Or he could seek out a lender who would place less emphasis on income. That meant he would have to pay slightly higher interest rates, even though the loan was fully collateralized.

If a lending institution could give him 75 percent of his $140,000 equity, he would have $105,000 to put toward another property. Lenders usually hold back 25 percent on rental property purchases, because that gives them a cushion should they have to foreclose on the property.

A $105,000 loan would be enough to purchase a small one-bedroom, one-bath condo in Sun City. John also did his homework and figured he could rent the property for $900 a month.

Instead of using a bank to fund this purchase, John used a credit union, which offered lower interest rates and no points. He secured a loan at 3.75 percent, which meant a mortgage payment of $486 a month.

John found a unit that sold for $104,000. He offered $100,000 in cash and the seller accepted. This property will not be as profitable as his first rental, but it cost $40,000 less.

Using the most recent appreciation and rental rate estimates for Sun City and a $900 a month lease, John estimated that in the first year of operation this one-bedroom property would generate $12,067 in equity (see Table 12.1, Columns B+C+D: $7,600 + $2,628 + $1,839). This is based on $781 in monthly expenses and a cash flow of $219 a month.

At the end of ten years, the one-bedroom property will generate $161,913 in equity, compared with $255,594 for his first rental. His total gains will be $417,507, and the total value of his investments will be $657,507.

Not too shabby for just two properties.

If he owned two more properties, he could reach $1 million in a decade.

That's all it takes.

But where should John go from here?

He has two options.

First, to really grow his portfolio, he needs to maximize his return on investment (ROI) by leveraging other people's money. Up to this point, John has been putting his own money up, primarily because his income is too low. But after a couple of years of leasing and sound business decisions, lending institutions should be more generous to him.

The second option he has is to do a 1031 Exchange.

Using Other People's Money to Maximize ROI

When using your rental properties as collateral for another purchase, your goal is to put as little down as possible on your next purchase. You want to leverage other people's money, because that leaves you equity to purchase other properties, and that in turn is the fastest way to achieve financial freedom.

Table 12.1
Expected Gains from John's Two Rental Properties in 10 Years
Based on Past Appreciation and Rent Price Trends in Sun City, Arizona

Column=	A		B		C		D	
Year	Gains by Year (B+C+D)		Equity from Appreciation (7.6% Per Year)*		Cash Flow (4.3% rent increase per year thereafter)**		Equity from mortgage payments***	
	2-Bed	1-Bed	2-Bed	1-Bed	2-Bed	1-Bed	2-Bed	1-Bed
1	$19,181	$12,067	$10,640	$7,600	$6,282	$2,628	$2,259	$1,839
2	$20,363	$12,828	$11,449	$8,178	$6,552	$2,741	$2,362	$1,909
3	$21,623	$13,640	$12,318	$8,799	$6,834	$2,859	$2,471	$1,982
4	$22,966	$14,507	$13,255	$9,468	$7,127	$2,982	$2,584	$2,057
5	$24,400	$15,433	$14,263	$10,187	$7,434	$3,110	$2,703	$2,136
6	$25,927	$16,423	$15,346	$10,962	$7,754	$3,244	$2,827	$2,217
7	$27,557	$17,480	$16,513	$11,795	$8,087	$3,383	$2,957	$2,302
8	$29,295	$18,610	$17,767	$12,691	$8,435	$3,529	$3,093	$2,390
9	$31,151	$19,817	$19,118	$13,656	$8,798	$3,680	$3,235	$2,481
10	$33,131	$21,108	$20,571	$14,693	$9,176	$3,839	$3,384	$2,576
Totals	$255,594	$161,913	$151,240	$108,029	$76,479	$31,995	$27,875	$21,889
Total Gain=	$417,507		$259,269		$108,474		$49,764	
Total Values=	$657,507		$499,269					

*The 7.6% estimate is derived from data compiled by Zillow for the previous 10 years and is compounded.
**The 4.3% estimated appreciation rate is derived from Zillow and is compounded.
***30-year fixed rate mortgage loan at 4.5% interest. The original loan amount is $140,000 and amortization tables were used to calculate the interest and principal payments.

The less equity you put into a property, the higher the return on investment (ROI).

The formula to calculate leverage for a property is simple: divide the investment property financing amount by the property value. This is also known as the *loan-to-value ratio*.

Here's an example.

Let's say property values are increasing at an average of 6 percent per year and you want to purchase a property that costs $100,000. You refinance your rental property or obtain an equity loan for $50,000.

If you put all of that money down on your next purchase, you have 50 percent leverage, or a 50 percent *loan-to-value ratio*.

At the end of the first year, your property is worth $106,000 ($6,000 + $100,000). Your net gain is $6,000. So, your return on investment (ROI) is 12 percent ($6,000 ÷ $50,000).

Not too shabby. (And we haven't even added in principal payments on the mortgage.)

Now let's say you put down only $25,000 and finance $75,000. You have 75 percent leverage and your net gain from appreciation is still $6,000.

But your ROI now is 24 percent ($6,000 ÷ $25,000).

And, best of all, you have $25,000 left over to purchase another property.

If you purchased another property right away, your net gain would be $12,000 instead of $6,000.

As I've noted before, leverage explains in large part why many people have gotten wealthy through real estate.

Depreciation and Capital Gains Taxes

If John sold both of his properties at the end of ten years, their fair market value would be $499,269. That amount includes the $240,000 he spent purchasing the two properties and $259,269 in equity from appreciation that he earned on them (see Table 12.1, Column B).

If he did not reinvest the proceeds, he would have to pay two taxes on that sale.

He would pay a 25 percent recapture depreciation tax and a 15 percent capital gains tax.

The recapture tax would be 25 percent of $95,636 (the total amount of depreciation taken over the ten years for the two properties), or $23,909. [53]

Ouch!

The capital gains tax would be even higher: $38,890 ([$499,269 - $240,000] x .15).

Double ouch!

In other words, John would have to pay $62,799 in taxes on the sale. His profit after taxes would be $196,470 ($259,269 - $62,799).

That's a 181 percent net return on investment ([$240,000 + $196,470] ÷ $240,000).

That's nothing to cry about.

John will have to pay capital gains taxes when he sells.

But there is a way to eliminate the recapture tax.

First, he could move into one of his two rental properties and if he lived there for three years or willed the property to his daughter, there would be no depreciation tax on that property.

The second alternative is to purchase a more expensive property under a 1031 Exchange and then sell that property. That wipes out the depreciation tax on the first two rentals.

You read that right: *It wipes out the depreciation tax.*

Doing a 1031 Exchange

As noted above, if you sell your property without buying another property, you'll pay capital gains taxes as well as a depreciation recapture tax. That could mean a tax bill of 30 percent or more on the profits.

---

53 I used a depreciation calculator available at https://www.calculatorsoup.com/calculators/ financial/depreciation-property-realestate.php/

But invest that money into a more expensive property and you can eliminate the recapture tax as well as defer your capital gains taxes, thanks to what is known as a *1031 Exchange* (also known as a "Starker Exchange").

The term is defined under Section 1031 of the IRS Code, which allows an investor to defer paying capital gains taxes as long as another "like-kind property" is purchased with the profit gained by the sale of the first property.

A like-kind property is defined broadly. You can exchange a single family rental property or a duplex, commercial office building and apartment community, or any other combination thereof. The only requirement is that the purchase price and the new loan amount for the replacement property must be the same or higher than for your original property.

> **Fact #18**
>
> *There are four ways to do a 1031 Exchange: simultaneous, delayed, reverse, and construction.*

When you sell the first property or properties, your proceeds are held by a "middleman" who uses it to purchase the replacement property for you.

There are four types of exchanges:

- *Simultaneous.* This type of exchange means the replacement property and relinquished property close on the same day at the same time. Any delay can disqualify the exchange and full taxes can be are assessed.

- *Delayed.* This exchange is the most common and occurs when the *exchanger* relinquishes the original property before acquiring the replacement property. The exchanger has 180 days to buy the replacement property.

  The exchanger secures a buyer for the original property and executes a sale and purchase agreement before the delayed exchange is initiated. The exchanger hires a third-party exchange intermediary who holds the proceeds from the sale in a binding trust for up to 180 days while the exchanger acquires a like-kind property.

The exchanger has forty-five days to identify the replacement property.

- *Reverse.* This is also known as a *forward exchange*, which occurs when the exchanger acquires a replacement property through an exchange accommodation titleholder before identifying the replacement property. In other words, you buy first and pay later.

  Reverse exchanges are done in cash, which means many banks won't do them. The exchanger must decide which of her or his investment properties are going to be acquired and which will be "parked." Failing to close on a relinquished property in 180 days will result in a forfeit of the exchange.

  The exchanger has forty-five days to identify which property is going to be relinquished and must complete the sale of the replacement property in the remaining 135 days.

- *Construction.* This exchange allows investors to improve the replacement property by using the exchange equity. In other words, the exchanger can use her tax-deferred dollars to enhance the replacement property while it's under the control a qualified intermediary for the remainder of the 180-day period.

  The replacement property must be of equal or greater value when deeded back to the exchanger. The improvements must be in place before the taxpayer can take the title back from the qualified intermediary.

Most investors used a delayed exchange.

My summary of a 1031 Exchange is simplified. Most investors, even seasoned ones, need experts to make sure they comply fully with the law. I strongly recommend you seek professional advice if you're considering a 1031 Exchange.

So, to sum up, if you do a 1031 Exchange, the depreciation recapture tax on the property you sell is wiped out. You begin depreciating your new rental property and will have to pay a recapture tax when you sell it. But if you sell within a year or two after the purchase, the recapture tax is small.

You must hold onto the 1031 property for at least one year before selling it. The IRS does expect that your intent in purchasing the new property was for investment purposes, not for avoiding paying the recapture tax.[54]

Reducing Your Capital Gains Tax

I just discussed how you can reduce your depreciation recapture tax.

Is there a way to reduce your capital gains taxes?

Yes, two ways.

First, keep your income under the $434,550 threshold. The capital gains rate is 15 percent under that amount and 20 percent over it.[55]

Second, you can reduce your capital gains taxes if you move into one of your rental units or move back into a home that you once lived in and have been renting.

For example, let's say you purchased a rental unit eight years ago and rented it out for six years, and then you moved into it for the last two years. When you sell it, you can exclude 25 percent of your gain from taxation, a percentage that is equal to the amount of time you spent living in it (8 years ÷ 2 years = 25%).

> **Tip #31**
>
> *To reduce your capital gains on the sale of a rental property, consider moving into it two years before the sale.*

In order to qualify for the reduction, you must own the property for at least five years.

If the sale of a property pushes your income over $434,550, which means you'll have to pay a 20 percent capital gains tax rate instead of 15 percent, ask the buyer to spread the sale of the proceeds from your property over two or more years to keep your income in the 15 percent bracket.

---

54 See opinion from Asset Preservation Incorporated, retrieved October 22, 2019, from https://apiexchange.com/how-long-to-hold/

55 Some high-income taxpayers also are subject to an additional 3.8% Medicare tax on net investment income.

Chapter Thirteen

Step 10: Further Your Education

John is thinking about selling his properties through a 1031 Exchange. He'd like to pick up a small apartment complex, maybe a fourplex. (Buying and maintaining small multi-family units is the topic of my next book in this series.)

Of course, he could continue to buy single-family rental units. If he had two more properties, he estimates he could quit working his part-time job.

But he's having fun and enjoys a good challenge.

So John's new goal is *to buy a small multi-family unit in Sun City or a nearby area within the next year.*

In the meantime, he's reading all he can about multi-family real estate investing. And he's teaching his daughter how to manage the rental property business.

After your first rental property purchase, chances are you, too, will revise your goals.

That's a good thing.

And as your goals change, your needs for information and knowledge change.

Educating yourself about the real estate investment business doesn't mean you need to get a college degree or a real estate license. In fact, many of my wealthy real estate friends never attended college and don't have a license.

But all of the successful people I know have one thing in common:

They never stop learning.

To achieve and maintain financial freedom, they continually educate themselves, through reading, research, and professional organizations.

The Importance of Education

To be honest, I didn't really understand the importance of education when I started college. In fact, I wasn't even sure my decision to go to college was a good one.

Most of my friends who stayed home took jobs at one of three big corporations in Everett, Washington, and they were buying houses, cars, and boats and were getting married and having children.

I envied them, at least a little.

I was a "poor" college student and they were buying fun things, even though most of the stuff they bought was financed and they were in debt.

They wanted financial freedom.

But they didn't know how to get there.

At the time, I didn't know either.

But in hindsight I can see that the greatest thing I learned in college was simply the value of learning and education. I majored in business, which gave me a basic understanding of how business worked and how to conduct basic research. I learned to think more clearly and began to view education as a life-long process, not just a four-year degree.

> **Tip #32**
>
> *To thrive in a free-market system, you have to continually educate yourself.*

The value of education and learning took on even greater significance years later, when two of the major manufacturing companies left Everett and some of my friends lost their jobs.

To thrive in a free-market system, you have to continually educate yourself to keep yourself valuable.

And the layoffs in Everett taught me another important lesson: *When you work for*

> **Tip #33**
>
> *Being your own boss is the best way to secure your job.*

someone else, you can never be sure you have job security. Being your own boss is the best way to secure your job.

The Value of Personal Development

In addition to educating themselves on real estate, the successful people I know also emphasize *personal development*—pausing now and then to take stock of where they've been and where they want to be, as an individual and a business person.

I learned much of this from a college football coach, Frosty Westering, who was a professor of physical education at Pacific Lutheran University in Tacoma, Washington, when I attended.

He was a great coach.

In fact, he was the winningest coach in the history of the National Association of Intercollegiate Athletics, which represents smaller colleges and universities. His teams won two national football championships, and in terms of winning percentage, Frosty is ranked among the top ten coaches in all college divisions.

But he was more than just coach.

Frosty taught me and other members of his team the importance of having a positive attitude.

He was an expert in what he called *Positive Mental Attitude* (PMA).

His theory was simple: *If you develop a positive attitude, you are more prepared to take on the challenges of life.*

Frosty gave me my first experience with "personal development," which I define as *a lifelong process in which you assess your skills and qualities, consider your aims in life, and set goals to maximize your potential.*

My second experience with personal development came at age twenty-one, when the police pulled me over after I had been drinking and driving. The court made me go to classes,

> **Fact #19**
>
> *Personal development is a lifelong process in which you assess your skills and aims in life and set goals to maximize your potential.*

and in those classes I met a woman who encouraged me to do a "family intervention" with my father, who drank more than he should.

My family and I intervened and he quit drinking.

Just like that.

The power of personal development played out before my eyes.

There are tens of thousands of books, articles, blogs, podcasts, and videos offering advice and knowledge about the real estate business and about personal development. I even have an extensive library of information at my website, www.KenMcElroy.com.

I strongly encourage you to explore personal development programs that will help you not only in your business, but in your personal life as well.

Real Estate Investing Resources

In addition to the published literature on real estate, there are scores of organizations and associations that represent various types of investors and professionals in the real estate business.

Here are two major ones that focus specifically on the real estate rental property business.

I also include a list of websites associated with my companies and with the Rich Dad Advisors series.

1. The National Real Estate Investors Association (https://nationalreia.org) is a nonprofit 501(c)6 organization and has a number of local chapters. It offers not only educational materials and seminars for its members but discounts on products and services at stores like Home Depot and Office Depot/Office Max.

NREIA has 40,000 members and represents local investor associations, property owner associations, apartment associations, and landlord associations. The organization says it is the "largest broad based organization dedicated to the individual investor."

Its mission is "to develop, support and promote local real estate investor organizations while serving the interests of the real estate investment industry through networking, education, support, leadership on legislative issues, and promoting professionalism and standards of excellence in our industry."

NREIA argues that "real estate is the safest, surest way to financial security."

I can't argue with that.

As a condition of membership, each group in the NREIA is required to adopt the NREIA Code of Ethics, which includes banning the practice of artificially inflating the value of any property, failing to disclose to any buyer conditions that would knowingly reduce the value of a property, taking advantage of new investors' trust of seasoned investors by over valuing estimates, and deceiving any other NREIA club member.

When you visit the main website, the organization will refer you to local organizations near where you live. After you join one of those organizations, you can sign up with NREIA.

2. American Apartment Owners Association (www.american-apartment-owners- association.org) bills itself as the largest landlord association in the country, with more than 110,000 members in the United States. The Association is actually a privately-owned corporation, and I wouldn't list it here if it did not offer a free membership.

The group caters to landlords who own both single- and multi-family units and offers a variety of services including extensive tenant screening, credit checks, landlord forms, rental applications, and relevant real estate updates. AAOA's stated mission is *to provide superior property management services that will equip landlords to better manage their investment properties.*

The organization offers more than thirty landlord forms that can be downloaded and printed. It offers instant tenant background screening services. Its website also offers a list of vendors that can offer home improvement services, apartment repairs, remodeling, and other services.

AAOA also keeps its members informed about the latest real estate news through its free e-newsletter and its website. Its online archive is available to the public.

Conclusion

Congratulations on learning the key concepts provided in this book. You have taken an important step toward your financial independence. Best wishes in all your investing endeavors.

Ken McElroy

Online Resources Affiliated with Rich Dad Advisors

Books and Information for Investors and Entrepreneurs
www.RDA-Press.com

Real Estate
www.KenMcElroy.com
www.McCompanies.com
www.McCompaniesInvest.com

Asset Protection and LLC formation
www.sutlaw.com
www.corporatedirect.com

Tax Planning
www.wealthability.com

Paper Assets – Stocks and Options
www.thecashflowacademy.com

Sales Strategies
www.salesdogs.com

The Rich Dad Company
www.RichDad.com

Appendix I
Summary of Text Boxes

Fact Boxes

Box #	Fact	Chap	Page #
1	Horatio Alger novels promoted wealth and the American Dream.	1	3
2	Being born to rich parents is the fastest way to wealth, but real estate beats all the other paths.	2	7
3	Rental properties can be depreciated even though they usually increase in value.	2	16
4	Equity drawn from real estate is exempt from taxes.	2	19
5	The rich get richer because much of their income is taxed as a capital gain, not as regular income.	2	20
6	Two advantages of investing in real estate: You don't have to quit your job and you don't have to be an expert investor.	2	22
7	A Limited Liability Company (LLC) protects your personal assets.	4	44
8	Three key drivers of rental market supply and demand are employment, resources and location.	6	70
9	The Fair Housing Act provides fines and monetary damages against landlords who discriminate.	8	105
10	Five valid reasons to evict a tenant include nonpayment of rent, lease violation, crime or drug-related activity, property damage, and expiration of lease.	8	112
11	Most small businesses use the cash method of accounting, which is simpler than the accrual method.	9	118
12	The standard-mileage deduction for use of a vehicle for business is nearly 60 cents a mile.	9	123
13	Real estate professions get a tax advantage: They can deduct losses from other income.	10	128
14	Section 179 of IRS rules allows large ticket items like refrigerators, computers and stoves to be fully deducted in the year they are purchased.	10	132

Table Continued on Next Page

15	You will need to issue a 1099 form to any contractor to whom you pay more than $600 to in one year.	10	133
16	Historically, rent rates have risen faster than inflation.	11	148
17	Rent rates tend to increase as mortgage rates increase.	11	149
18	There are four ways to do a 1031 Exchange: simultaneous, delayed, reverse, and construction.	12	163
19	Personal development is a lifelong process in which you assess your skills and aims in life and set goals to maximize your potential.	13	169

Tip Boxes

Box #	Tip	Chap	Page #
1	Wealth gives you freedom.	1	4
2	To be financially free, you need motivation, a good work ethic, and a willingness to learn.	1	5
3	A depreciation recapture tax on rental property can be eliminated if an investor invests the proceeds from a sale into a more expensive rental property.	2	18
4	A 1031 Exchange allows you to cut depreciation recapture taxes and defer capital gains taxes.	2	21
5	To be financially free, you need to be a lead dog and educate yourself.	3	32
6	Read books about real estate investing and seek the advice of knowledgeable people.	3	33
7	Goals can and should change as conditions change.	3	37
8	Financial freedom often can be achieved in a decade or so.	3	39
9	You don't have to pay someone to setup your LLC, but seek professional advice if you have questions about complying with the law.	4	45
10	An idle asset is better thought of as a liability.	5	53
11	Debt is good when you leverage other people's money to invest in real estate and make money.	5	54

Table Continued on Next Page

12	House hacking (living on your rental property) is one of the easiest ways to purchase your first rental property.	5	58
13	A rent-to-own contract can give you time to repair your credit and generate enough equity to cover the down payment.	5	60
14	The market is more important than the property.	6	69
15	Look for markets where supply of rental housing is low and demand is high.	6	69
16	Diversity in businesses and resources generally creates more stability in a market.	6	71
17	Zillow, Trulia, Realtor.com and other online real estate websites are good places to start researching a market.	6	72
18	Many counties with metropolitan areas offer online sites where citizens and investors can obtain tax and assessment histories of properties.	6	74
19	If you are buying a home for rent, be sure the deed covenants and homeowners associations allow rentals.	6	75
20	You may not need an accountant or attorney on your first rental property purchase, but as your business grows you will need a team to help you make good decisions.	6	76
21	Mortgage payments on small rental properties should be no more than two-thirds of the total rent payment.	7	77
22	Hiring a property manager company works best when you a strong cash flow.	7	87
23	Your relations with tenants should be cordial but professional.	8	99
24	A well-maintained property will reduce your risk to lawsuits.	8	100
25	A tenant background authorization application is your best tool for selecting good tenants.	8	102
26	Be sure your lease agreement addresses everything: If something is not in the contract, it does not exist.	8	108
27	If your tenant fails to pay rent on time, you must impose a late fee to ensure they understand the contract must be enforced.	8	110

Table Continued on Next Page

28	Bookkeeping is very important. Don't ignore it.	9	117
29	Consider refinancing your rental properties in three to eight years, when enough equity has accumulated.	12	147
30	Small increases in rent can amount to a lot of revenue over time.	12	152
31	To reduce your capital gains on the sale of a rental property, consider moving into it two years before the sale.	12	165
32	To thrive in a free-market system, you have to continually educate yourself.	13	168
33	Being your own boss is the best way to secure your job.	13	168

Myth Boxes

Box #	Myth	Chap	Page #
1	The stock market is the fastest way to wealth.	2	8
2	You have to be wealthy to invest in real estate.	2	23
3	You don't always have to put money down to purchase property.	2	24
4	You need to spend your own money to buy apartments and commercial property.	3	38

Definition Boxes

Box #	Definition	Chap	Page #
1	Financial freedom exists when your income is sufficient enough that you no longer worry about your finances.	1	4
2	Return on Investment (ROI) refers to the effectiveness of an investment.	2	9
3	Cash flow is the amount of money that flows into and out of your business.	2	13
4	Leverage means using other people's money (OPM) to make money	2	15

Table Continued on Next Page

5	Equity is assets minus liabilities, and debt is a duty to pay someone.	3	15
6	A goal is something you plan to achieve.	3	35
7	A D-U-N-S number is used to track credit for a business.	4	50
8	A home equity line of credit (HELOC) has no closing costs and is a fast way to get cash, but the interest rate can be higher.	5	55
9	An adjustable rate mortgage (ARM) typically offers a lower interest rate, but the rate can be increased when market conditions change.	5	55
10	A traditional mortgage has closing costs but typically offers the lowest interest rate.	5	56
11	In a contract for deed, the seller becomes the lender.	5	59
12	"Being in escrow" is a contract in which a third party, often a title company, receives and disburses money or property for the transacting parties.	5	61
13	Passive income is income received on a regular basis, with little effort required to maintain it.	5	62
14	An accredited investor is a person or organization with substantial assets or income.	5	63
15	A business plan is a promotional flier and is needed to raise capital from accredited investors.	5	64
16	A proforma financial statement makes estimates of future expenditures and income.	5	64
17	A purchase agreement is a sales contract – an offer to purchase a property.	7	88
18	A warranty deed is a document in which the seller guarantees he or she has a legal right to transfer title to the a buyer.	7	90
19	Due Diligence is a time period in which the buyer investigates the property's physical and financial condition.	7	91
20	A lease agreement spells out the responsibilities of tenants and landlords.	8	105
21	Tax deductible expenses include interest payment, utilities, supplies for repairs and maintenance, and use of vehicle.	9	121
22	Depreciable expenses include loan closing costs and remodeling expenses.	9	122
23	Double-entry accounting creates a balance sheet based on actual costs rather than market values.	9	125

Index

R

real estate professional, 27, 72, 128-130, 137

reduce costs (how to), 152-153

refinance loan(s), 157

Rent and Royalty Income and Expenses, 128

rent-to-own agreement, 60-61

rental rates, 14-15, 71, 84, 148-150

rental inspection checklist, 108

repairs, ix, 16, 61, 75, 81, 94, 100, 107-108, 121, 123, 129-132, 136, 138, 140-141, 150, 154, 171

reserve/contingency fund, 81, 124, 141

retire/retirement, 53, 57, 127, 129

return on investment (ROI), 9, 12, 14, 26, 159, 161-162

return on investment, 9, 14, 159-162

revenue(s), 5, 13, 36, 63, 86, 117, 119-121, 148, 152, 155

Rich Dad, Poor Dad (book), 44

Rich Dad Advisors, 52, 170, 173

risk/risk taking/credit risk, 16, 22, 24, 27, 31, 49, 51, 58, 60, 64, 69, 90, 93-95, 100, 104, 155-157

S

savings and loans, 58

Schedule E, 128

Scottsdale, AZ, 49, 52, 67, 71, 123

Section 179, 132

secured credit cards, 50

security deposit, 104, 106, 108, 110, 121, 130

seller, 28, 39, 59-60, 62, 72-76, 86-91, 94-95, 119, 123, 131, 140, 156, 159

sewer, 75, 81, 86, 91, 101, 107, 131-132, 136

shareholder(s), 44

short-term returns on investment, 28

single entry method of accounting, 124-125

social security, 39, 47, 48, 129, 135

sole proprietorship, 43, 47, 49

standard-mileage deduction, 123-124

Start Your Own Corporation (book), 52

start-up expenses, 122

stock market, 5, 8, 13, 15, 34

stocks, ix, 7-9, 13-16, 21-22, 24, 26-28, 120

sub-letting, 106

Sun City, AZ, 38, 67-68, 72-75, 77-78, 80-87, 94-95, 137, 139, 156, 158-159, 167

Supplemental Income and Loss (Schedule E form), 128

supply of rental housing, 69-70

About the Author
Ken McElroy
Author, Principal and Co-Founder of MC Companies

Ken McElroy has nearly three decades of experience in multi-family asset and property management and development. MC Companies is a full-service real estate investment and property management group that since 1985 has developed, built, and managed multi-family housing communities. Currently the group owns over 8,000 units in several states, including Arizona, Texas, and Oklahoma worth more than $1 billion in real estate assets.

MC Companies believes in Sharing the Good Life with its communities through donations and volunteering time to support various local and national charities. MC Companies Team members annually donate more that 2,500 hours to local and national charities. Ken sits on the Board of Directors for the Southwestern Autism Research and Resource Center. For two years, he was the Walk Chair for Autism Speaks Arizona, an organization he has been involved with for over 14 years. MC Companies also supports the Cystic Fibrosis Foundation, Hydrocephalus Association, The University of Arizona Health Sciences Center, The Leukemia & Lymphoma Society, Susan G. Komen for the Cure and many more.

Ken is the author of the best-selling Rich Dad Advisor Series books *The ABCs of Real Estate Investing, The Advanced Guide to Real Estate Investing, The ABCs of Property Management,* and *The ABCs of Buying Rental Property* as well as *The Sleeping Giant* and *Return to Orchard Canyon.* He is also a contributor to *The Real Book of Real Estate* by Robert Kiyosaki and *Midas Touch* by Donald Trump and Robert Kiyosaki.

Best-Selling Books in the
Rich Dad Advisors Series

Get more books by Ken McElroy
Jumpstart your dreams with these inspiring and informative reads:

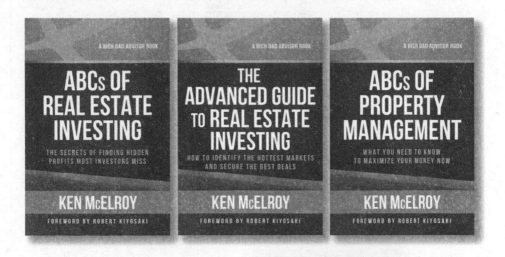

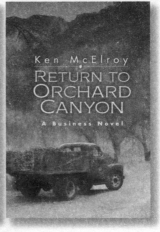